INSIDE OUT EMPATHY

EXPLORE THE UNDERESTIMATED *SUPERPOWER* ESSENTIAL FOR BUILDING, DEVELOPING, AND INSPIRING A ROCK-SOLID TEAM.

ERIN THORP

 # CRetreat2019

EThorp

Publishing Services provided by Paper Raven Books
Printed in the United States of America
First Printing, 2017

Paperback ISBN = 978-1-7751463-0-8
Hardback ISBN = 978-1-7751463-2-2

TABLE OF CONTENTS

To my parents,
thank you for your courage,
your vulnerability and
for showing me there is no
easier, softer way.
I'm forever grateful.

"When you show deep empathy towards others, their defensive energy goes down, and positive energy replaces it. That's when you get more creative in solving problems."
—Stephen Covey, Author, Educator, Businessman, Speaker

INTRODUCTION

Welcome. With deepest gratitude and humble respect, thank you for choosing this book. I've written this book with two intentions. The first intention is to introduce, explore, and outline the merits of leading with more feeling, more connection, and more understanding, by sharing my story. The second intention is to offer the leader in you some tactical and practical suggestions so that you can start leading with empathy immediately. Along the way I will explore potential pitfalls and challenges you may face if you try to "turn off" or ignore your emotions.

You've likely been a leader a lot longer than you think. Whether you are an eldest child, an only child, or one of many children, you started developing and utilizing skills and talents that allowed you to lead your life. Yes, leading starts in childhood.

This book is part self-exploration and part how-to guide, blended together and filled with the words I wish I had available years ago. One might argue that I wouldn't have been ready to hear the message and understand the meaning back then, which very well might be true. But you are not me. You may be ready to hear these words today, and, if not, they will stay with you until the day you are ready. This is the power hidden in the words. Maybe you already have the context in which to apply the teachings in this book. I write to start a conversation, demystifying the "touchy-feely" emotions inevitability involved in leading people and to find harmony with the objective, seemingly detached process of leadership: targets, goals, action plans, schedule, and budgets.

Leadership is a complex and dynamic topic, primarily because people are complex and dynamic beings. And with leadership all around us—parents, teachers, managers, coaches, politicians, captains, bosses—rarely do we give our own style and approach much thought. Have you ever asked yourself and explored the answer to the question, "What is my style?" or "How could I be more effective?"

Leadership is evolving, because the world is changing. Corporate structures are changing, entrepreneurs are on the rise, and there are more multi-level marketing and home-based business opportunities than ever before. All of this opportunity is demanding more leaders and more from leaders. If people aren't satisfied in a role or on a team, gone are the days where they feel trapped. They simply adapt, shift, and move on, as the opportunities are endless. Off they go, searching for a spot where they will feel utilized, challenged, autonomous, and fulfilled, to a place where they have a purpose. Now is the time for a new style of leadership to emerge in order to make our teams more stable and effective, and to nurture the people we encounter in the workplace, in social circles, and at home.

In the recent past, companies used to rely on homogeneous hiring practices to staff their teams with people who were all relatively the same. For instance, I work in the engineering field, where you typically find a lot of detail-oriented engineers being led by a more senior detail-oriented engineer. Recent research is proving that diverse staffing, featuring a range of race, gender, and age, as well as skill sets and attitudes, is a lot more effective at producing tangible, bottom line results.

Over the past 10 years, I've seen a shift in how teams are being built and structured. We're starting to see teams of people who are skilled in engineering, sales, management, and other proficiencies, and we're starting to see leaders who lack technical savvy but have an ability to lead. Leadership is now starting to be seen as a distinct and separate expertise.

This shift in perspective, with a focus on diversity, is true of new and emerging businesses. Now, entrepreneurs are finding employees or freelancers who are just as diverse in skill sets as they are in geographic location, gender, race, religion, and socio-economic background.

It's a trend that is also emerging in our social circles and families, where our friends are different from each other and our children are different from each other. This is a reality I live and breathe every day in my own household with three incredibly beautiful and unique children. The increased diversity creates a richness in our communities, companies, friendships, and families. Our teams are more effective, our friendships are more fulfilling, and our family relationships are deeper.

When life was more homogenous without the far-reaching influences we have today, we didn't have to worry about developing varied leadership skills quite as much, because leading people who are just like ourselves is, quite frankly, not that difficult. And, as we include and encourage increased diversity (which is, again, a worthy and worthwhile effort), we find that we need leadership that can make the most of this diversity.

It is my belief that empathic leadership behaviors are the way forward in an increasingly diverse world.

Empathy is made up of both innate traits and learned skills, which combine to help us forge deep connections with others. Fields traditionally dominated by females—assistants, nursing, teaching, caregiving—have relied on both these innate and learned empathic abilities in their leaders for centuries, while male-dominated corporate culture has historically had no place for such traits. This book is a call to action, to bring these traits to all teams in all situations, regardless of the dominant leading gender.

For the purposes of this book, it's important to understand what empathy really means and how it fits in with similar emotional abilities.

Sympathy is an understanding between people, sharing common feelings, or feelings of pity and sorrow for someone else's misfortune.

Compassion is the response to the suffering of others that motivates a desire to help.

Empathy is the ability to see and share in the emotions of others.

If you're reading this book, you're likely feeling called toward empathic leadership. Perhaps, like me, you've been feeling out of place for years, working on fixing your emotional landscape to fit into current corporate culture. Maybe you have the innate quality of empathy, or maybe you're curious about how to develop empathic skills. Either way, you've noticed that there might be a better way to lead teams, and this book will help you navigate the way.

I am the eldest child of four siblings and have been leading myself, my family, and my colleagues for the better part of three decades now. As a Professional Engineer and Leadership Coach, with 20 years of experience as both an indirect and direct leader, I have seen firsthand how an empathic approach to leadership can build high-performing teams, create engaging culture, and drastically improve results in a very short period of time. I've also seen how a lack of empathic leadership proves unsustainable and ineffective, even if it is successful in the short-term.

I hope to help you discover the leadership qualities you've had all along, right from childhood. Perhaps there is something about you that you've always wanted to change. For me, it was my emotions. I thought I was broken, after years of performance evaluations where the primary piece of feedback I received was that I was "emotional" and needed to learn to fix myself. If you've had similar thoughts of wanting to change and wondering if you're broken, let me show you how I turned one of my greatest perceived weakness into my leadership superpower!

You will see through my experiences and stories how leadership can be felt by both the leader and the team, and how to cultivate your desired culture. We will explore why this topic is important, defeat some damaging myths, and dig into the nuts and bolts of teams.

As important as it is to know your own strengths and weaknesses, leadership isn't about what you, as a leader, need. Leadership is about what your team members need to get things done. Leadership is about them and not about you; it's about using your understanding of your own skills and experiences to meet people where they are.

Empathy underlies all successful leadership strategies, and I will show you how you can incorporate it directly into your company, your relationships, and your family. I will walk you through what it looks like to have and practice empathy with others and with yourself.

"With great risk comes great reward." It's a phrase that is often tossed around without much thought. I see no greater risk than sharing myself with another human being, so does it not stand to reason, then, that in sharing myself—my story, my feelings, my thoughts, my beliefs, my skills, and my challenges—we all can reap the reward?

I have written from my own perspective and experience.

While my message is not limited to women, it is who I had in mind while writing this book. I write for the younger me who so desperately needed these words to know that she belonged, she was worthy, and that she was not broken. I believe there is something for everybody in these pages. Please, join me. I'm so glad you are here.

A CALL TO A NEW VISION OF LEADERSHIP

"A comfort zone is a beautiful place, but nothing ever grows there"
—Unknown

The first step in solving any problem is recognizing that there is a problem. I believe we are in the midst of a leadership crisis, and I am no longer able to stay silent, sitting quietly in my comfort zone, without at least trying to make a tiny bit of difference in this world.

Whether you have yet to fill a formal leadership role, have been newly promoted to a leader position, or have been in the seat for many years, we all need to rally behind a new vision of leadership, one with more heart, more connection, more honesty, and deep vulnerability.

Welcome to part one of this book. In this first part, I want to explore what it means now that you've been called to lead, to share a bit more about me and how I got here, and to extend an invitation to join me on the quest for engaging our emotions, specifically our empathy, to lead with passion, purpose, and power.

CHAPTER 1:
YOU'VE BEEN CALLED TO LEAD, NOW WHAT?

"If someone offers you an amazing opportunity and you're not sure you can do it—say yes—then learn how to do it later."
—Richard Branson, *Philanthropist, Entrepreneur, Investor*

You're a leader now.

OR

You've just been told you will be promoted.

OR

You've decided to go out on your own, start your own business, and be your own boss.

OR

Your side hustle has just turned into your full-time gig, and you now have a team of highly motivated, ambitious, dedicated people looking to you for their next move.

Doesn't matter how you got here. You're here. And you may have no idea what you've just gotten yourself into. Fears, self-doubt, and panic are all starting to rise up inside you. You can't help but think, "Now what?" or "Am I really ready to do this?"

Take a breath. Yes, you are ready. You've got this. Armed with an ability to learn, a genuine curiosity, and a couple of new skills and tools of the trade, the transition to effective leader can be made with ease and grace.

Let's face it, the skills and abilities that made you stand out as an individual contributor may not necessarily be the same qualities that set you up to be the inspiring, visionary leader you picture in your mind.

If you try and enter the leadership space doing the same things you were doing in your role as a team member, you will likely experience some major bumps and bruises along the way. In extreme cases, you may even fail at leadership.

Now, this is not to scare you off; rather, it is to let you know that you will need to invest in yourself. You will need to learn new skills, try new approaches, and generally open yourself up to vulnerability like you've probably never done, if you want to succeed like I think you do.

A few of the things I had to learn along the way (some of which might surprise you) are:

- How to move from a "do-er" to a "lead-er."

- How to build the map and plan the expedition, not just carry a backpack and follow directions.

- How to understand and articulate to your team, that the work you are asking them to do fits into the big picture and why they should care.

- How to listen deeply and probably to at least some stuff that doesn't really deeply matter to you.

- How to be flexible, yet strong.

- How to be open, yet focused.

- How to care about results and care about people at the same time.

- How to teach people that it's okay to make mistakes as long as there is growth.

You are now in charge of creating and defining the culture of your team, business, or organization. What do you want that to look like? What are your rules of engagement? What behaviors will be acceptable or unacceptable? Your team is watching your every action taken or not taken, your every word spoken or unspoken. What is it you want them to see?

I want people to see me as an authentic, compassionate leader with the capacity to lead a diverse range of skills and abilities. But I certainly didn't start out like this. I will share my story with you in the next chapter, and you'll see that I used to be a dictator, a "my way or the highway" kind of leader. I can honestly say that, had I stuck with that style of leadership, I wouldn't have made it to this point in my life successfully, either in my career or as a wife and a mother.

It has been a journey in learning to trust my own abilities and skills, while I also open up and allow others to share and explore the path forward with me. It took years of working on listening—really active listening—to be able to hear what people say and don't say, and it's a continuous process (I still work on practicing this skill every day).

So where does one start? Leadership starts with you, and you need to know more about you than anyone else does. You need to become the expert in all things that make you, you! To start, you will need to explore your deepest desires and your darkest places, and you will need to challenge almost everything you know to be true at this very moment. Some of the current beliefs you have will move forward with you, while some will be left behind. You will discover parts of yourself you've never given voice to, and, I hope, bring them into your present. My wish is that you are constantly and curiously exploring your own edges, and challenging your own perspective.

Your leadership journey doesn't begin when you get your first job as a leader, or when you take on your first volunteer position on a board. It begins as soon as you're born. In fact, you're already well into the journey, whether or not you know it. We develop leadership abilities from childhood, so in order to more fully understand your strengths and weaknesses as a leader, you've got to start at the beginning. To illustrate how you might go about this in your own life, I'm going to take you on my own journey from the beginning, and open up about what I've discovered. I'll highlight your own strengths and weaknesses as a leader by excavating parts of my own deeply personal journey.

We cannot be effective leaders of others until we can effectively lead ourselves. I will challenge you to look deeply, to unveil parts of yourself you likely keep hidden away from the world, and I will invite you to embrace empathy as one of the many tools in your leadership toolbox.

The first step to changing anything is the desire to change something.

CHAPTER 2: MY JOURNEY

"Maybe the journey isn't about becoming anything. Maybe the journey is about un-becoming everything that isn't really you, so you can be who you were meant to be in the first place."
—Unknown

Learning Command and Control

I was born on a September day in the mid-seventies, the first born child of my parents. I'll never know if being born under the sign of Virgo and being the first born significantly impacted to my leadership journey. At the very least, what I do know is that these details are a part of my journey.

My mom, Loreen, and dad, Patrick, were farmers, and at this time, just starting out in the dairy business. How my name came to be was likely my first encounter with "sponsorship." My mom, a child of the 1950s and a self-admitted hippie, drew the logical conclusion that because I was born in the fall and we lived on a farm, that her firstborn daughter should be named Harvest. I'm not sure what life would've looked like having the name Harvest. I think about it often, as I'm introducing myself or as I see my name in print on a business card, and I think maybe it would've been pretty cool. I, however, was not meant to be a "Harvest," as my dad stepped up and said, "No child of mine is going to have a name like Harvest." Sponsorship is defined as the vouching for or backing up of another person, being responsible for someone's growth, development, education, and professional learnings, and parents are their children's first and most important sponsors.

I learned a lot from my mom and dad over the years, watching them adjust to each new addition to our family, living values of honestly and courage and always supporting each of us kids in whatever way we needed.

When I was two years old, shortly after my second sister, Danielle, was born, we moved from a rural farming community in northern Alberta, Canada to a fishing town in rural bush Alaska. It was a town named Bethel, along the mouth of the Kuskokwim River, near the Bering Sea. There remain only two ways in and out of the town: by boat or by plane. My dad was there to help his brother run a small chain of retail stores along the river. My mom, a psychiatric nurse, went to work in the social services system.

We lived in Alaska for seven years, from the time I was two years old, until I was nine. In 1980, we flew home to Alberta early for Christmas so that my youngest sister, Lesley Anne, could be born in Canada. I used to get extreme motion sickness as a kid, and when we would travel, my mom would always buy me a brand-new purse to go with my outfit. This shiny, new, and usually patent leather purse is what I would throw up into as the plane landed. My mom could casually and quietly dispose of it on our way out of the airplane. I remember feeling as a kid that I just wanted to make this easy for her. I hated this part of myself. I didn't know why I had to be so difficult and why I couldn't just be like my sisters.

In 1983, my little brother, John, was born in Alaska. I remember sitting in the hospital waiting for him to be born. I was six at the time and I remember waiting with Danielle, who was five, for our new sibling's arrival. We didn't know at the time whether we were having a new brother or sister.

I remember taking care of my brother as an infant, wrapping him up in blankets and carrying him all over the house. I fed him, bathed him, and watched him grow. To me, this was just part of being an older sister, but I can now appreciate that my parents were likely struggling to take care of all of us. As an adult, now with a family of my own, I can empathize more and more with what my mom and dad must have been going through, being so far away from family and having four young children under the age of six with no real support. I also think about living in a town that you can't leave except by boat or plane and realize how isolating that must have felt.

It was during this time, my parents' addictions to alcohol and narcotics became unmanageable. They could no longer keep ignoring it, trying to maintain the status quo. One day, in late March 1985, my mom's friends came to her, staging what I now know to be an intervention. They explained to her that she could not keep doing what she was doing; if she couldn't do it for herself, she had four little kids and a husband she needed to think of. I remember my mom recounting the story of the day this intervention was staged and how she fought back, saying she couldn't understand how she was supposed to leave her family for 28 days. How would the kids and her husband ever get through this? She told her friends that my dad wouldn't be able to find his socks without her. Her friend asked, "Well, was he wearing socks when you met him?" My mom replied, "Of course, he was! What's that got to do with anything?" Her friend looked at her and simply said, "He'll find them again, Loreen. You need to save yourself."

So off she went to Anchorage, Alaska to a 28-day live-in treatment program. My sisters and I were talking recently, and we actually don't remember her being gone for this month. At the time, I was seven years old, my sisters were six and four, and my little brother was one. This is the first story in my life I can remember where someone put themselves first with the goal of saving themselves so that they could give to others. While I officially had to step into a mom role during that month my mom was in treatment, I realize now that my journey as a leader started the day I was born. And it does for each of us.

As I sit and write these words, I wonder about a few things. Why has it taken me almost four decades to realize the lesson of saving yourself first, that putting yourself first, before others, is in service of others so that you can give more? I also wonder how many other kids are stepping forward as leaders in their families, their classrooms, and their peer groups without the support, guidance, and tools to help them strengthen and flourish.

My memories of Alaska are, ironically, quite exciting. We got to travel by snowmobile down the frozen river and have campfires in the bush. We were often taken care of by loving Eskimo elders who fed us all kinds of strange (but yummy) food and dressed us in furs and other beautiful handmade things; the Mukluks and Kuspuks we wore as children were truly something to be cherished. Summers were filled with days of endless light and winters were nights of endless darkness. As a kid, you're not affected by these things the same way as an adult—it was fun to be where your imagination could soar—but as an adult, I can't imagine being a mother of four small children and not seeing the sun for a few months every year.

It was during this time in Alaska that my entrepreneurial spirit started to emerge. There was a bachelor who lived above our house in an apartment, and I used to do his laundry for a quarter a load when I was six years old. I also did the family laundry because that needed to be done. I had begun to see things that needed to be done around the house and voluntarily stepped into the space to get them done. No one was asking that I take on so many chores. I was doing them out of a desire to be helpful. I don't remember a time in my life where I saw things that needed to be done (gaps, missing pieces, holes in the fabric of the family, or a business, or a team) and didn't step in and fill them.

In early April 1985, my dad visited my mom at the treatment center after her detox, and he came to the realization that in order for them to stay together, things needed to change. While he never attended a treatment center, he did come to terms with his addictions and began living sober. He noticed how much my mom had transformed and knew that he would have to follow the same path if we were going to be able to stay together as a family. My dad had been married twice before and openly talked about how he was tired of leaving families behind. He knew that he, too, would have to confront his addictions in order to keep us together. So he and my mom began their journey, with the help of a 12-step program, and started living sober one day at a time, together.

My parents realized that they needed a better support network, and they had a farm waiting for them back in Alberta, with family nearby who would be able to help with all of the children. (After we moved, they founded a 12-step group in our small town, a group that is still active today and is a beautiful part of their legacy.)

As my parents grew and changed, learning how to be vulnerable and honest with those in their lives, they also started to be more responsible in their family roles. This caused me to become confused and angry. I was struggling to find my place, to truly be in my role. I was used to taking care of a lot of the details of raising a family when my parents were sick and unable, and now they were stepping on my toes, taking over my territory. I didn't understand why they wouldn't let me continue to do the things I was good at doing. It felt like it was a slap in the face, like I wasn't good enough to do these things anymore. And I struggled to find my place in our family. I didn't know how to be a kid or how to let go of the responsibility of being a parent. I was still seeing all of these gaps, all of the things that needed to be done, and I wanted to be helpful and get them done.

When I was 10 or so, my mom began working away from our family home in an indigenous community in northern Alberta, to support our family. This left my dad at home with four young kids, trying to farm with occasional childcare help from our grandparents. It was easy for me to slip back into the role of being a mother, taking care of my brothers and sisters, making sure that dinners were made, and that laundry was clean.

During this time, my dad did his best meet the needs of three daughters who were now in their early teenage years. There were a lot of crooked ponytails that didn't quite match, and if we wanted braids, we had to go to grandma's house the night before to get those done. In seeing that someone needed to know how to braid hair, I started to pay attention to how my grandma did it, and eventually learned how to do it myself. My sisters and I also taught ourselves how to curl our own hair, long before YouTube and the Internet. (We had a few instances of crooked haircuts and minor burns, none of which were too pretty, but it was all in the spirit of being helpful.)

I wanted so desperately to be helpful to Mom, and to take on some of the load. I look back now and chuckle, because, oh my gosh, it's entirely possible that all we did was create more work for her with something else! I have never fully appreciated or valued the decisions both of my parents made to support our family and raise us during these years. I am honored to have been a part of their story and to have them as a part of mine.

What I realize now is that I never stopped to think about how it made people feel when I did their job for them. I had no self-awareness, which is not unusual for a child. My intention was honorable, therefore I thought, it should have been accepted and even celebrated. I had no idea how I was being perceived by my family and my friends. I became extremely results and task-oriented. If I could do it—faster, better, sooner, quicker— then I would. I would demand that things get done my way. And by my teenage years, my command-and-control leadership style was well developed and thriving.

Once I was able to drive, I started driving my siblings to events, always in the spirit of sharing the load of raising four children. I, once again, began to fill in any space available. I was never scared and never backed away from a challenge. I wanted people in my life to be happy, and I thought that if I could take over and do things that needed to be done, it would make them happy.

As my siblings all moved into their teenage years, I continued to view myself as being responsible for them, but I started becoming more and more resentful of them. I saw them playing with their friends, attending parties, trying out and playing for school and club sports teams. They tested the limits with alcohol and drugs, which my parents firmly guided them in, but also allowed them to explore the space and test boundaries. I never realized at the time that I was allowed to do all of these things as well. I just didn't do them, nor did I ever ask if I could. I created the barrier that said I couldn't do it.

As I look back on the years I was living at home and growing up, I remember feeling misunderstood. Why couldn't people see that I was just trying to help? Why couldn't they see and accept the help I was willing to give?

It wouldn't be until many years later, that I would finally understand that it wasn't the help they were unwilling to accept, it was the approach to the situation and style of leadership in which I offered the help. I was trying to lead with my inherent leadership skills of dominance, control, and command, which wasn't what the situation required. Unless you are in a critical situation—war, the operating room, or a crisis situation—control and command leadership is often ineffective. Most situations have the luxury of time to explore, to consider different and contrasting points of view, and to collectively determine the best path forward, because the situation doesn't demand a quick, conclusive decision. I just didn't know any other way to lead with my limited skills and abilities as a teenager.

Entering the Corporate World

As I neared the end of my high school career, it became evident that I would need to choose what I was going to do with the rest of my life. I had spent so much time focusing on everyone else. that I hadn't given much thought to my own life.

One day, I wound up in the office of my high school guidance counselor, who had been there for so long that he had counseled my mom 21 years earlier. It should have come as no surprise to me then, when I, a girl from a farming community, showed up and said, "I want to go to university. What can I take?" that he replied, "Well, would you like to be a nurse or a teacher?" I told him I didn't want to be either. I don't enjoy working with little kids (which seems ironic now that I have spent the past 17 years raising a family), and I really can't stand the sight of blood and the thought of working in healthcare didn't light me up.

The school counselor was taken aback and seemed shocked by my answers; I really don't think he knew what to do with me. He suggested that I do an aptitude test in his office, so I spent an hour and filled out the forms, and answered the questions. Lo and behold, what came out, after all of this well-spent time, was that I had an aspiring career as a taxicab driver or food and beverage server ahead of me. I knew that neither of these options was the career choice for me. After wasting almost half of my morning in his office, I asked him if I could borrow the calendars for the University of Alberta in Edmonton and the University of Calgary for the weekend. He said yes, and I walked out with two thickly-bound paperweights, headed home for the weekend.

I remember flipping through these books, looking for any faculty that would accept me into an undergraduate program. I was looking for a program that did not require my English or Social marks, because these were my two least favorite subjects in school and my lowest grades. I also was acutely aware that I needed to be employable after receiving a bachelor's degree. I didn't think that I would have the luxury of masters programs or graduate school, such as law school; my parents were farmers and wouldn't be in a positon to pay for this education. I was already having to take on debt from student loans, and knew I would have to get a job after four years. Armed with this criterion, it quickly became apparent that engineering was one of the only choices that I had; my love of physics and calculus had finally paid off. I applied to the faculty of engineering in the fall of my grade 11 year and by the following spring, I had been conditionally accepted into both engineering programs. All I had to do was make a choice. One school was about a two-hour drive from the farm, and the other was about five hours away. Which to choose?

Most of my high school friends who went on to post-secondary education ended up attending the university closer to home. I remember distinctly thinking that I needed to be farther away than that. I needed to get out into the world and meet a new group of people. I was beginning to become aware that if given the choice, I picked the road less traveled.

In the fall of 1995, my parents moved me five hours away into the University of Calgary residence. I had been placed on an all-girls floor but had never met my roommate, and knew only her name from the information packet the school had mailed me earlier that month. I was extremely excited to be there but had very little insight into what everyone one else was feeling, including my parents. Here I was, waving happily out of the window, feeling excited and nervous and full of opportunity, but they were feeling loss, grief, remorse, and uncertainty as they drove away. My mom tells a story of how they were so visibly upset that they made the gas station attendant cry when they stopped to fill up for gas on the way back to the farm shortly after dropping me off.

That first year wasn't easy. I was often homesick, and it forced me to get to know myself as an independent person, not as a big sister or a caretaker. For the first time in my life, I was only responsible for me. This would take a few more years (okay, maybe decades) to sink in. Of course, I fell into some of the same default roles that I had played in my past and quickly became the caretaker and the "mother" of the all-girls floor. I would drive us around, make sure everybody got home, make the Halloween costumes, organize the pot luck dinners, and generally ensure that everyone was safe and cared for.

But I also made an effort to try new experiences. I went out and had a little fun. For the first time I enjoyed going to parties with new friends and classmates, volunteering around campus, hiking, impromptu road trips, listening to music, going to movies, and exploring this new city I now called home.

In 2001, at the age of twenty-three, I graduated from university with my degree in civil engineering and was hired as the project engineer/construction manager for a commercial construction firm. Even though I hadn't grown up around construction sites, my farming background lent itself well to this career path. My dad never treated me or my sisters any differently than my brother or the hired hands on the farm; we operated the same equipment and had similar responsibilities during planting and harvest, and when working with the cattle. The construction site felt a lot like the farm, and it felt like a natural place for me to be. I knew the results I needed to get, the schedule and budget to do it in, and the team to get it done. I never found it intimidating that my entire team was men who were usually older than me and far more experienced. I had a job to do, and I was hired to do it. Somebody trusted me enough to do it, and come hell or high water, I was going to deliver on those results. I was going to show them that I could do this job.

I have always taken on my work with a high degree of responsibility, and I have held an extremely high bar for myself in terms of expectations, which has served me well in my career in terms of getting results. The one roadblock I kept running into at this early part of my career was my emotions. I couldn't figure out how to turn them off when things got stressful or didn't go the way that I had planned or anticipated. And, more often than not, I would find myself crying in my office or, God forbid, in my boss's office. I was completely embarrassed and ashamed that I couldn't control my emotions and just tough it out.

If I'm being honest, I really wasn't a great listener during this time. I didn't try to put myself in other people shoes, because I was too caught up with wanting them to be in my shoes. I wanted them to understand what I was going through, and often wondered why they couldn't see what aspects of this project needed to be done and just get it done for me. It would take me another decade to learn and implement the "seek first to understand, then to be understood" habit from Steven Covey's famous book, *The 7 Habits of Highly Effective People.*

I also met and married my husband, Matthew, during these years. As both of our careers became more secure, we decided it was time to start a family. However, the stress from my job and from being a new wife, combined with my lack of coping skills and not knowing how to take good care of myself, ultimately lead to a very long (and not so happy) year of trying to get pregnant. That year drained me, physically and emotionally.

Eventually, though, our daughter, Olivia, was born in May 2004, and after 10 months of maternity leave, I decided to return to work. I had an arrangement where I would go into work at 6:00 am, Matthew would drop off Olivia at daycare, and I would leave work by 3:00 pm to pick her up. This lasted for about two and half weeks before I heard people in the office talking. One day, as I was walking out of the office (having been there for nine hours already), I overheard some comments about "being a part-timer" and "cutting out early," insinuating that I was not pulling my weight. That was likely the biggest trigger anyone could have touched on for me.

I was ill-equipped to have a conversation to address this type of chatter head-on, and I remember thinking as I walked out that day, "I don't need this! I do not have to put up with this. It's time to start looking for somewhere else to be. These people are never going to change. This is construction and its 'old boys' club mentality is never going to change. I need to be somewhere where I am supported because I want to be there for my family."

I realized that if I wanted to see change, I needed to participate in it and be a part of the solution, so I began looking for another position. I wanted something with flexibility, possibly working from home, somewhere I wouldn't be watched over, where the outcomes mattered more than the minutes spent at my desk. And I found it.

Starting to Understand Myself

In my next career move, I landed a technical sales position. The company had a defined culture, a concise and truly lived-by set of values, where they invested in training their people. My first three weeks on the job were an intensive boot camp, where all the new trainees learned about the company, the products, and ourselves. This new company walked the walk and talked the talk. Culture was not just a poster on the wall, but was a publicly-declared set of values that aligned with daily practice.

One of the first things I had to do was complete the DiSC assessment, a personal assessment tool that identifies your prevailing behavioral tendencies. The test (either online or on paper) asks a series of questions, each with four possible answers, ranging from 'most' like you and 'least' like you. The end result provides you with insight into your dominate behavioral traits and communication style, either at home or at work, depending on which version of the test you are taking. (While the results often differ for work and family contexts, I discovered that my pattern of behaviors and communication were relatively consistent in both environments.) When used widely across an organization, the assessment provides a common language for your group, team, or organization, ultimately facilitating an increase in productivity, collaboration, and communication.

The results can be broken down into four quadrants, which represent the two basic motivators of our behaviors: our motor drive or 'pace' and our compass drive or 'priority.'

Pace refers to how we make decisions, talk, and think, and is broken down into two speeds: fast or slow. Are you a fast talker and fast decision-maker, or do you like to take your time with decisions, and choose your words after careful thought and consideration?

Priority refers to what we value and can be broken down into two categories: tasks or people. Task-oriented people care about getting things done and checking items off the list, and they tend to be highly analytical. People-orientated individuals care more about the people than the accomplishment, and they prioritize the feelings and experiences of the team over the tasks that are getting done.

I'm going to state the somewhat obvious here—there is no right or wrong pace or priorities. This is a tool to help you better understand yourself and your team. A team full of fast-paced, task-oriented people will function just fine, as long as no one with a different set of motivators ever joins the team. As soon as you introduce someone who isn't like the rest of the team, there will be discomfort and misunderstanding. The DiSC tool allows you to build a common language in your team, so that individual differences can be celebrated and integrated.

What does D-i-S-C stand for anyway?

'D' represents dominance. Key behaviors include the ability to see the big picture, and bluntness in expressing views and opinions. People who orient from this place of dominance willingly accept challenges and like to get straight to the point. So much so, that they may not ask how your weekend was, take time for 'small talk,' and could come across as insensitive. High 'D' people place emphasis on accomplishing results, the bottom line, and confidence, and are fast-paced, task-oriented team members.

'I' represents influence. Key behaviors include high levels of enthusiasm and optimism. People who orient from the place of influence love to collaborate, and generally dislike being ignored. They care about how the team is feeling, are usually the social organizers, and could be called the glue of the team. High 'I' people place emphasis on influencing or persuading others, openness, and relationships, and are fast-paced, people-oriented team members.

'S' represents steadiness. Key behaviors include a dislike of rushing, taking time to complete tasks, and a calm manner and approach. People who orient from a place of steadiness dislike change and are often the rocks of the organization. These are the people who have been there for years in the same role, doing the same thing, and are still motivated and excited to come to work every day. They love having the answers and demonstrate supportive actions to their peers and colleagues. High 'S' people place emphasis on cooperation, sincerity, and dependability, and are slow-paced, people-oriented team members.

'C' represents conscientiousness. Key behaviors include independence, objective reasoning, and a keen attention to detail. People who orient from a place of conscientiousness fear being wrong. This coupling of fear of being wrong, with attention to and love of detail, means that these individuals are slow to engage in a conversation or argument; however, once they have their position, they are rarely wrong. High 'C' people place emphasis on quality, accuracy, expertise, and competency, and are slow-paced, task-oriented team members.

Hopefully, now you can see that we need everyone! All types are necessary and important, and there is no one right way to be; we just are who we are. And we can use this information to our advantage when building and maintaining teams.

So how does this pan out in real life? Well, if a 'D' and 'C' are in a heated discussion or argument, the 'D' will *think* they are right and the 'C' will *know* they are right.

Can you guess what my profile looked like at this point in my life? You probably won't be shocked to hear that, in those early days, in every possible way, I was the highest 'D' you could possibly score, and everything else basically did not register on the scale. If you look at some of the descriptions of the high 'D,' you'll hear words like overbearing, domineering, autocratic, assertive, and aggressive. While this was certainly hard to hear, I knew it was true for me. It was the first time in my life I felt like somebody had held up the mirror, and I could actually see how others perceived me.

This discovery was critical in my journey. Often, we think the world perceives us in the same way we perceive ourselves, but we can't move forward in our self-exploration and really learn to embody change, until we give up this notion and seek to understand the ways in which the world perceives us. After hearing the results of the assessment, I finally understood that the way in which I was trying to get things done was not working in either my professional life or my family life.

I look back at this time, these three weeks in June 2005, as the first time I had become open to new possibilities. I was now aware of a different way to lead, and realized that I had a choice in how I showed up and how I got results. I finally understood that I could choose how I interacted with my peers, my husband, my parents, and my siblings, and that this choice influenced the outcome.

Fast-forward to September 2006 and our next child, our first son, Henry, was born. By the spring of 2007, I was ready to go back to work. I was offered a promotion to move into a project management role for one of the sales divisions. With the position came additional training and enrollment in the leadership academy at this company. I was introduced to the basics of leading others: how to select members for your team, how to handle performance management, and how to have difficult conversations. This training took place as a series of one-week sessions over the course of the next two years. These courses were taught in a classroom and then reinforced in the field by the behavior and the actions of everyone in that company.

Not only was my career as a leader growing, but our family was growing too, and my journey into motherhood deepened. My husband and I had to navigate moving from just the two of us, to just the two of us, plus one, and then the two of us, plus two. While I wasn't directly leading a team at work yet, I was indirectly responsible for supporting, influencing, and driving the sales division business. My skills as a leader were developing. However, they were not ingrained, nor were they embodied yet. I found it much easier to apply these rules of leadership to other people—to my teams at work, to my kids, to my husband (with limited success)—to anyone but myself.

In my personal life, I still expected people to do what I asked, when I asked it. I had yet to make the connection that people are people, no matter where they show up in your life. But I had become more aware that people are whole people, that we don't separate ourselves from our home life when we come to work, and we don't separate ourselves from work when we come home at night. Even if a professional environment has an undertone of "leave your work at the office and your personal life at home," I'd begun to understand that these slices of ourselves are always present and influencing our mood, behaviors, and actions, whether we know it or not.

When we try to separate our leadership journey into work or home, outward or inward, we often miss a huge piece of the picture, leaving us with 10 missing puzzle pieces and wondering why the picture doesn't look like we thought it would.

Effective Communication in Action

Around this time, Matthew and I decided that we would leave our city life behind and build a house on an acreage nearer to where I grew up. My parents gave us some land, and our family of four moved in with them for 10 months. Matthew took a year off work and built our house. It was during that time that I really got to see the differences in our approach to tasks and communication. I'm thankful for many of the discoveries early in my career, especially around communication styles, as it helped me understand how we were communicating with each other and how we were making decisions.

One of my most vivid memories of this time was picking out new appliances for the house. My list of requirements was short and sweet: black; a convection, double-wall oven; a dishwasher with no buttons on the front because we had very small children, and I didn't want them turning it on all day long; and a fridge that had the freezer on the bottom.

That's it. That was my list. I had no brand loyalty, no specifications, no warranty preferences, no performance data, nor did I care about any of this. We walked into the appliance store together, and I was ready to purchase that day. All we ended up doing was looking and asking for all the catalogs to take home. We left with a stack of books and no appliances. I could feel myself starting to get angry, frustrated, and resentful. Why couldn't we just buy the appliances I wanted to buy? Why did we have to go through all of this research, when I knew what we would end up with?

Of course, it didn't help that I was anxious to move out of my parents' house and into our house. I didn't want this process to take a long time, and yes, I was extremely impatient. I wanted it to go my way. I wanted to be done quickly. Get in, get out, make a decision, get it over with.

I don't know how or why I went back to the teachings of the DiSC profiling, but I'm so thankful I did; I'm sure it saved us in that moment. I began to understand that Matthew, who is a high 'C,' is exactly the opposite of me. He loves details, and he only makes a decision when he knows he's right. He doesn't just think he's right, like I do most of the time. Research, for him, brings excitement and enjoyment. Even though that idea is still hard for me to understand, I have learned to appreciate his love of research and to see how it contributes to the good of the family. Getting to that point, however, was a process.

I knew that it wasn't my job to change him, so how could I make the most of this difference between us to help strengthen our relationship, rather than allowing it to create a wedge between us? My answer was to embrace him doing the research, even if it meant a few extra weeks for us to arrive at the decision of our appliances. Six weeks later, we went back and ordered the appliances. Everybody was happy. We both got our needs met, and the decision was made together. This was probably one of the first times that I had ever used a professional teaching in my personal life, and I was amazed at how the two complemented each other. I had always thought that you needed to keep the professional and personal parts of your life separate, and never should the two cross. It was my first experience where I was consciously aware that I was whole, and that the professional and personal aspects of my life actually worked better together. Ten years later, I have a collection of many more experiences that reinforce this idea.

A Leadership Test

Thomas was born in late 2009 and completed our family. As I was preparing for my return to work after my third maternity leave in 2010, my company offered me the position of technical sales manager, leading a team of 12 engineers in western Canada. I had doubts about whether I was capable of leading a team that large, but I felt motivated by the challenge. I had confidence in the company's supports and structures, particularly the common leadership language we all shared, and felt reassured that those would provide a solid foundation to help me as I learned how to be a leader. Formerly, I had been a peer among the members of the team I would be leading, which created some anxiety about how the team would receive me as their leader, but I had to believe that we could navigate our way through the transition together.

The team I ended up leading was the same one I was hired onto five years earlier. And, as fate would have it, I also ended up leading my former colleague and mentor, Ryan. We were friends outside of the office; our families knew each other, and we looked after each other's clients during vacation and work travel. I didn't always agree with his approach to work, and, up to this point, I had been able to overlook these differences. Now that I was accountable for the performance of the team, I knew I wouldn't be able to look the other way.

Ryan had always operated outside the accepted work culture by making his own rules. His lack of regard for the accepted targets, and his unwritten agreements with former leaders, had led to performance challenges that the whole team knew existed but did not address. I remember sitting in my car on my first day as the phone calls started rolling in from the team members, as they found out who their new leader would be. For the most part, the team members seemed excited and offered congratulations, but I felt like I had an insurmountable mountain to climb in confronting the situation with Ryan. My integrity would not allow Ryan to carry on as he had in the past. I recognized the overall lack of respect for leadership in the group and the lack of trust between team members, which was exacerbated by keeping on an underperforming team member who apparently had a different set of rules to follow. I could not lead a team with low trust and respect, and I knew that confronting the source of the problem would be difficult.

It was my job to set the culture, to enforce those written and unwritten rules of conduct, and to set the expectations for behavior. Ryan had a history of behaviors that set him up as the outlaw of the group. It was widely known by the members of the team that Ryan created his own targets and metrics by which he was measured, and that he often chose not to adhere to targets and metrics set by the company. He showed up late for meetings, missed meetings altogether, dialed in late to conference calls, and was constantly unavailable to his sales team. Up to this point, Ryan had always been led by someone who lived in another city, which granted him autonomy to run his own show. But when I took over, I was familiar with Ryan's city, clients, work history, and even his family.

It became very clear to me early in my new role, that the team was watching me to see what I was going to do about Ryan. They all resented the fact that a double standard existed, with one set of measures of success for Ryan and another set for everyone else. Resolving the situation was going to be challenging, to say the least, and I had no idea how I could change this person and get him back on track.

After a conversation with my leader, I figured out that I didn't need to change Ryan; in fact, I couldn't change him. People have to want to change, and their situation has to be uncomfortable enough that they are willing and able to try something new. What I needed to do was clearly communicate the expectations and the challenges with the current behavior, and help him see a different way forward. I would need to clearly outline the consequences and inform him that his progress would be monitored. He had been with the company for over a decade and had some long-standing customer relations that the organization viewed as valuable, so I was hopeful that we would be able to work together to move forward in a positive direction.

I started to spend days with Ryan, as I did with all the members of my team. I needed to gather examples of current behaviors and situations from my time with him as his leader, and to not rely on my experiences with him from our time as peers. This was a critical step. Relying on experiences with former peers as a foundation for actions as their leader is a dangerous trap, and an easy one to fall into. While you probably do have valuable insight, watch out for "I know what it was like to work with this person, therefore I know what needs to be done as their leader." (If you find yourself in this situation, I urge you to try and start over with the whole team. You will need to re-establish relationships, and position yourself as their leader and not their peer.)

Consistently, Ryan would plan only a half day of work, would show up late, and would cancel just before we were scheduled to meet. He was often unavailable to his team members, who started to call me for the support they required. It didn't take very long for me to observe all the behavior I required. It was time to start a formal corrective action plan to encourage and coach Ryan, to meet standards of performance to which everyone else on the team was being held.

I worked with the human resources (HR) team and my leader to formulate the plan, and set up a time to meet with Ryan. He canceled at the last minute by email. We rescheduled. He canceled again by email. This pattern kept up for a while, until I drew the line in the sand and said that if he missed another meeting, he would be terminated immediately.

When the time came to meet, I chose a public place (a coffee shop) on purpose. Even though I do not often feel intimidated or frightened by others, going into a difficult conversation, like a poor performance review, is handled best in a setting with other people around. Calling someone else to join the meeting, especially when the individual may be resistant to hearing what you have to say, offers security and, at the very least, a witness to the exchange. As this was one of the most demanding responsibilities of my career, I needed to take care of myself.

He showed up to this meeting, which was a good start. I offered my observations and explained why his behavior in these observed situations was unacceptable, and I outlined the ways in which his behaviors negatively impacted the business and our team. I was rooting for Ryan during this conversation, hopeful that he would be able to see the impact of his actions, and that he would accept the coaching I could provide him. But at the end of the conversation, I was once again reminded of the lesson I had learned earlier: you can't change people. You can offer support, coaching, and perspective, but you cannot, and never will be able to, change someone without their willingness and desire to do the work themselves.

Ryan did not agree with my observations, nor did he expect me to follow through with the consequences I had laid out. I felt stunned that he was so resistant to change and, at the same time, felt a deep resolve to follow through on my obligations as a leader, to act with integrity and respect for myself, my team, and my organization while upholding the company's culture and behavior expectations.

We continued this cycle of corrective action performance meetings for a few months, and it was glaringly apparent that Ryan had no intention of changing. Much like my two-year-old toddler, he was testing my boundaries and waiting to see if I would enforce the consequences. I found myself in an incredibly difficult position, deeply aware of the impact my decision about Ryan's job would have on him and his family, but also deeply aware of the impact my inaction would have on my integrity, and our team culture and cohesion.

In the end, I had HR draw up the termination paperwork. Based on Ryan's unwillingness to listen in our performance discussions, I knew I needed additional support in the room when I delivered the news, and invited my HR partner and another leader from our organization to attend the meeting. Ensuring that I had support during this conversation was very intentional. I was the leader, it was my decision, and I was going to deliver the news. I wanted to own this part of the process and made it clear to my leaders that I would not shy away from the responsibility. It was terrifying and unpleasant, but highly necessary that I owned my decision and my role as the leader. Despite the fear I was feeling, I found the courage to step forward and act, and I am proud I did.

Ryan was shocked at the news that he was being let go. He genuinely believed that I wouldn't follow through with the stated consequences, and he turned angry and volatile during our meeting. I was thankful that I had the support around me and relied on their experience to help guide me through the process.

Thinking back to the moment I realized that I was going to have to let Ryan go, I had a hard time reconciling the situation and understanding the paradox of my own feelings. On one hand, the personal side of me saw that this team member was a breadwinner for a family with three small children at home, and I could empathize with him on that level. But the professional side of me didn't want somebody who didn't come to work, who was unreliable and untrustworthy, and who brought the team performance down.

During this whole process, I was a beginner, still in the early stages of learning with virtually no competence to do the work I knew was ahead of me; however, my commitment to myself and to learning the skills of a leader never wavered. The moment I had to step outside and see myself as someone the team needed for support was terrifying, but I asked for what I needed and found mentors and leaders who were willing to guide me through this very unusual situation. In other words, I diagnosed myself. By utilizing awareness of my own skills and needs, I made sure I had the support I needed to successfully navigate the situation.

I believe that this is the recipe for successful leadership. It starts with you. Can you diagnose yourself correctly before you start to diagnose others? Can you really put yourself in the other person's shoes? If you can begin to imagine what it must be like to feel their feelings and experience their world, you are on the path to making authentic connections, building trust, and inviting vulnerability into your relationships.

I learned a lot of lessons from the situation with Ryan early in my leadership career. I learned that, as a leader, you can't control, fix, or change anyone else. Chart the course, plan for contingencies, and leave it to the employee to choose the destination. My hope is that you find the destination that matches your charted course. For years, Ryan was allowed to drift along, and while the entire team saw this happening, nobody with the power to change anything took action. This performance pitfall will poison a team faster than any other workplace toxin, which leads to another lesson learned: a robust performance management system is essential and needs to be implemented at the very beginning.

Generally speaking, if you have team members who think alike, behave in similar ways, and are in the most appropriate role utilizing their strengths, things will run smoothly, and you likely won't need strong performance management systems. People will know what to do, get the job done, and everyone will be happy. However, when things are not running smoothly, especially in workplaces where you have a diverse team of people who think, act, and communicate differently, then a robust performance management system is required.

However, performance management cannot be implemented when things are falling apart; the performance management system must be in place prior to the need to correct performance. If you have a system in place to set expectations, offer feedback, and agree upon actions from the beginning, the likelihood of ever needing it to correct performance are slim at best. I'll explore performance management more in-depth in Chapter 8, but for now, think of performance as this simplified cycle: commit to the conversation, explore and offer the feedback, stay aware, repeat.

The one and only question that I can remember from a conversation with the company president before he approved my promotion into this leadership role, was, "If you agree to this role, you will likely have to make tough decisions regarding your former colleagues. Are you ready for that?" Of course, none of us really know if we are ready, but I said, "Of course I'm ready." I didn't know what he meant, nor did I have any inkling just how tough some of those decisions would be to make and execute. Looking back now, this situation was the one that pushed me outside my comfort zone further than I have ever been—as a person and as a leader—and is one I'm most proud of. I learned to trust myself—my skills, my abilities, and my emotions. My ability to feel into all sides of this situation allowed me to navigate this leadership test with integrity and grace.

CHAPTER 3: AN INVITATION

"After living with their dysfunctional behavior for so many years, people become invested in defending their dysfunctions rather than changing them."
—Marshall Goldsmith, *Author, Leadership Coach*

Having grown up surrounded by 12-step programs, the serenity prayer has become deeply engrained in my beliefs. Written by Reinold Niebuhr, it goes, "God, grant me the serenity to accept the things I cannot change, the courage to change the things I can, and the wisdom to know the difference." The words serenity, courage, and wisdom in particular have always stood out to me, and speak to me as an invitation to act.

I always start with courage, which is simply taking action despite the fear or resistance you may be facing. Since I was young, I have always been told that the only one I could change was myself. This annoyed me to no end during my teenage and young adult years, mostly because it was so true that it was hard to hear and accept. For me, having courage to change is actually having the courage to change myself. Whether it is a belief, an action, my mindset, my perspective, or one of my many habits, I have to have courage to change myself.

When I dig a little deeper and think about whether serenity or wisdom comes next after courage, it seems that wisdom wins out in almost every situation. I first reflect on what I might need to change—the courage to change is always my starting point—and, if nothing comes up, I feel a calm settling in, telling me that this where I need acceptance. Wisdom guides me between courage and serenity.

So here it is, my invitation to you. I invite you to have the courage to connect to yourself through the practices of mindfulness and empathy for the remainder of this book. I promise you it will not go unrewarded. It could get messy and perhaps sometimes painful, and that's okay. Take a breath and find the courage to keep moving through the resistance.

Connect to Mindfulness

When I look back to my childhood, I know now that I was just picking up on the emotions of everyone in my life. I didn't have the skills, knowledge, or the resources to be able to deal with all of those emotions. I had no language around emotional intelligence, or how to separate what I was feeling from what everyone else was feeling. When I would get too overwhelmed with people, I would focus on the results that needed to happen. Even to this day, if I'm not careful and don't remain completely conscious of my actions, feelings, and thoughts, I can end up in a place where I think, "If I just get it done, everyone will be happy".

The periods of my life when I've damaged relationships as a leader, both professionally and within my own family, have happened when I've slipped into a results-oriented approach only, instead of blending in the empathic, people-oriented approach.

The struggles between me and my mom were real, but it was because we were both battling from the same place of 'just let me do it.' She was the mother. She wanted to be able to take care of us. She wanted space to be Mom. And I now see the same struggle playing out between me and my own daughter. She's highly independent, very self-motivated, and enjoys stepping into the role of caregiver in our household.

She worries deeply about her brothers and her father and I, and at the same time, wants to be a kid, have free time and play dates just like her brothers. I don't know that I'll get it right, but I'm trying to help her navigate the space as she moves from child to woman.

At time of writing this book, I have been a mom for 13 years, and I can honestly say that not a day goes by that I don't struggle with 'doing it all'. I work daily on creating space for others to help me. The first step is to invite others to do so. Next, there must be space for people to help—real space, not passive aggressive, quasi space where help isn't really wanted. This approach of creating space and inviting help applies both personally and professionally, which is why I work on this practice daily in all aspects of my life.

I want my children to learn how to take care of themselves first. I want them to be able to feel their emotions, to articulate them so that others understand, and to have space for others in their life. At the same time, I also want them to be aware of other people. We have many conversations around these topics, and I am fully aware that I won't know the effectiveness nor the effect of these conversations for many years to come, but it doesn't stop me from trying. My children need to know how their actions and behaviors affect others and how small, simple adjustments can have deep, lasting results.

Just because I'm teaching my children about taking care of themselves, doesn't mean I've learned everything there is to learn. As an adult, I'm working on how to enjoy playtime and creating free time to spend with my children. I'm learning how to take better care of myself, so that I have more to give to others. And I'm figuring out that relationships are just as important as any task or result when stepping into a leadership role. Even when I volunteer at the kids' schools, I'm continuously amazed by how taking the time to build relationships helps the work get done almost effortlessly.

While the past plays a role in who we are and what we've learned, it does not dictate your future. Let me say that again. The past does not dictate your future. We get to choose in every moment going forward who we are going to be. We get to decide if the behavior we are choosing is serving us or limiting us.

This is my invitation to you, to move into a space of connection with yourself, those you love, and those you lead. Give yourself the permission and time to test and try on some new things, to make mistakes, to experience what works and what doesn't work, and to adjust in your role as leader.

Invite your team members (personal or professional) to a conversation about what they need, how they like to communicate, and what truly matters to them. Team members include anyone with whom you are trying to accomplish a goal, such as family members, children, professional colleagues, mentors, advisers, or volunteer committees; anyone on your team should be a part of the conversation.

The guiding principle behind empathic leadership is that there is no "one way" to lead, because each person is unique and each situation is distinct. We must engage with and know our teams so that we can respond appropriately and with higher effectiveness. We must be fully present and connect in the moment, and to do so, we must connect with ourselves first.

Connect to Empathy

As I continue on my journey, I am able to better understand why I continue to see teams of like-minded people, and why diversity is so hard to achieve. (For the purposes of this book, I define diversity as an understanding that each individual is unique and as a recognition of our individual differences along dimensions of race, ethnicity, gender, sexual orientation, socio-economic status, age, physical abilities, religious beliefs, or political beliefs, just to name a few.)

Left to my own devices and without conscious thought, I would unintentionally create a team of people who thought, acted, and behaved just as I do. The reason for this is simple: we can communicate easily with people like us and are better able to understand each other's perspectives and behaviors. But, if we build a team of like-minded and like-skilled people, we reduce our ability to innovate and are unable to push ourselves and others to achieve more. If I do not have a team with skills and strengths to complement my weaknesses, how can I ever do more than what I see as possible or what is already within my reach?

I didn't begin my leadership journey appreciating empathy as a skill to hone. In fact, in my early career years, I fought my own empathic reactions. I had always been told that I was too emotional, that I needed to learn how to have a poker face, that I should be tough. I had been trying to fix this perceived weakness for decades and was really getting nowhere. It wasn't until I read a piece on empathy that my thoughts completely shifted around what it means to be emotional.

Empathy is the ability to relate to people, to see and feel what other people are seeing and feeling.

Understanding empathy in this light transformed my own definition and perception of this ability I had. I was actually quite good at empathy; the ability to feel what other people were feeling, had been bringing up emotions for me for so long in my career. I just didn't understand that's what was going on. I began to realize that this was something I did not want to fix; rather, it was something I needed to learn how to channel and use to my advantage.

I already understood what each of my team members was feeling, when somebody was engaged or disengaged, when someone was on the fence, and who was highly motivated and ready to dig in to do the work. What I began to understand was that not all people have the highly-developed empathic abilities I had. I could leverage my abilities with other leaders, who could use my empathic approach to leadership to help them build high performing teams. Not only could I use it in my own leadership journey, but I could help other leaders in their journey.

Later on in the book, in Part Three, we will talk about practical ways to develop the skills required to be an effective, empathic leader, which you can implement immediately. In the next few chapters, though, I want to spend some time on why leadership matters at all, to describe what it feels like, to explore what's important to know about leadership, and to defeat the most damaging myths.

EVERYDAY EMPATHIC LEADERSHIP

"Leadership is about empathy. It is about having the ability to relate to and connect with people for the purpose of inspiring and empowering their lives."
—Oprah Winfrey, *Author, Actor, Media Proprietor, Philanthropist*

L eaders are present in our lives whether we want them or not, and whether we notice them or not. As humans, we have a natural and instinctual desire to follow. A few will forge ahead and go where others have not gone, and by the very virtue of this action, these individuals are leaders. Leadership matters because it happens all around us every day, in our families, work places, social circles, and communities.

Like most things, when we have good leadership, we don't make a lot of noise about it. Often we are even unaware of the fact we have good leadership. But when we have a bad leadership experience, we can't stop talking about it. Whether it's good or bad, it does take a lot of courage to be the one out front breaking new ground, standing up for ideas, teaching, inspiring, and coaching. Leadership comes with great responsibility. Intentional or not, the leader writes the rules of engagement, sets the expectations, and defines acceptable behaviors, which collectively make up a culture.

CHAPTER 4: UNDERSTANDING WHAT LEADERSHIP IS AND IS NOT

"Everything that irritates us about others can lead us to an understanding of ourselves."
—Carl Jung, *Psychologist, Psychiatrist, Journalist, Inventor*

It's time to explore what leadership is and what leadership is not.

Picture, for a moment, a parent walking with their child. What does it look like when a parent is in front? What about when a child is in front? When I'm walking with my kids, if I'm out in front, setting the pace and the direction we move, my kids will naturally follow. I don't have to work very hard to keep them with me, because they want to stay close to me. However, if I try to walk in the back, keeping them in front of me and herding them along, they scatter like cats. I'm constantly pulling the daydreamer back in line, yelling at the oldest to slow down, and hurrying the baby along to keep up. I'm scolding them for walking too slow, for not going in the right direction, and for not paying attention.

Leadership is being out front. Management is steering from the back.

Being "the boss" feels like being in the back, pushing your team in a direction, trying to get some people to speed up and some to slow down, redirecting to stay on course. In short, it's a constant herding of cats.

Being a leader feels like you're out in front, setting the direction and pace, without having to avoid tripping over anyone going too slow, or rushing to catch up with the speed walkers. Your team follows your direction and your vision, so you rarely have to correct course.

Sometimes people will get behind, lose their way, or even decide to leave when you're out in front. But if they are dedicated to your vision, and assuming you've got the right person on your team, this is usually easily remedied with a quick conversation, to understand what's holding the person back and providing the correct type of leadership and support to meet their needs.

There are a lot of misconceptions about leadership.

Leadership is not:

- Telling people what to do.

- Being right all the time.

- Having all the answers.

- Being the smartest, strongest, or most well-connected person.

Leadership is:

- Providing a path forward.

- Listening, not just hearing.

- Having a deep respect for differences.

- Demonstrating trust and integrity.

- Knowing how and where to find the answers.

- Pursuing self-improvement constantly.

- Asking for help.

Leadership is a pleasantly persistent pursuit of learning and growth. If you're telling people what to do, you're a boss, not a leader. When I think back to my early beginnings in leadership, even as far back as my interactions with my siblings, I realize how ineffective I was at truly leading. I incorrectly believed that I could be effective by demanding trust and respect, not earning it, and by telling people how to do it my way and demanding perfection, which was completely unrealistic and unattainable.

To be completely honest, I still fall into this trap today, especially when it comes to my own kids. I'm working to understand why I'm much more tolerant of a new team member learning a new skill on the job, than I am of my own children learning a new skill at home. It's almost laughable as I sit and write this down, how my expectations of my kids' abilities to clean the house is set at a level for someone who's been doing it for 30 years, rather than a level that is appropriate for a seven-year-old who just learned how to turn on the vacuum last week.

There is always something to learn, even if you've done the same task or had the same conversation twenty times before. Why? Because we are constantly growing and changing every day. The beautiful part of this cycle of constant growth and change is that, in every moment, interaction, and situation, we get to choose how we show up, how we behave, what we do and don't do, what we say and don't say.

Take a moment to pause and reflect. What has your experience been with your own leaders in your life? What has your experience been as a leader in your life? What choices are you making?

Inclusive Diversity

The word 'diversity' came onto my radar around 2010. The business case for diversity has been around since the 1960s, but it wasn't until this point in my career that diversity directly affected me. In 2014, I attended a conference where I heard one of the speakers give the following definition to Inclusive Diversity: "diversity is being invited to the party, inclusion is being asked to dance." I don't remember a single other speaker from that conference, but her words have stayed with me for years.

I love this analogy of dancing together, because it speaks to what it takes to build a partnership, to move in sync with each other. To dance with someone is to truly partner with them. By asking one to dance, we're inviting that person to share an experience with us, which allows us to be better understand and respect each other. It's the same with diversity and inclusion; if diversity is seeing and recognizing our differences, then inclusion is creating an environment built on the foundations of involvement, respect, and connection.

I have come to understand why inclusive diversity cannot be a "flavor of the month" topic but, instead, must become an ingrained part of how we build teams; it must be recognized as a necessary and vital part of leadership. Inclusive diversity requires that a leader, or organization, creates an atmosphere in which all people feel valued and respected and have access to the same opportunities; everyone has not only been invited to the party, but has also been asked to dance.

When we create teams, we will be more successful in reaching our goals if we have people on that team who have different skills, different opinions, and different behaviors. As leaders, our job is to teach, facilitate, and support our teams to work together effectively, to truly bring out the best in each other. And in order to create an environment that is rich with respect and where my diverse team members have access to the same opportunities, I need to be able to feel what it is like to be in their shoes. I must connect with my empathic abilities.

Any business owner, from large corporations to small businesses, must be aware of this phenomenon of building homogeneous teams full of like-minded people. I don't think we set out to do this on purpose. We do it, because it's part of our desire to belong, to be included, and to have things work easily. When you look around and study some of the most highly effective organizations and teams, they are not scared of diversity; they embrace and leverage diversity. Great companies and inspiring leaders have the ability to see everyone's differences as strengths, and utilize them with ease.

Gathering and leading a diverse team is not an easy path. It is a path filled with self-reflection, self-doubt, terrifying vulnerability, times of failing forward, and lots of adjustments along the way. I believe that the optimal way to steward a diverse team is to develop empathic leadership, the style of leadership that strikes the balance between the bottom line results and the people who make those results a reality.

How comfortable are you seeing yourself as a leader? Are you able to feel what it's like to be the person you're trying to lead? Can you understand what they're going through in their daily life? Do you have any idea of what it might take for them to get out the door and even arrive at the place of business, to sit down in their chair by 8 am? Do you have any idea what the demands are of them when they return home after working for you all day long? How aware are you of your own personal and professional demands and the impacts those demands have on your own ability to connect?

What expectations do you place on yourself?

Seeking to become a well-rounded individual is not the answer. All of us excel at some areas of our lives and truly struggle in other areas. This is by design. The human race as a whole is built to connect with each other; we are hardwired down to our DNA to form bonds, to build communities, and to live in groups. So why would we ever strive to be 'well-rounded' and able to do everything on our own? It goes against our very biological programming as a species.

So, it begs the question, why do we continue to hire teams of people who look and think and feel just like us? In my experience, these teams are the least equipped to perform. Homogenous teams are riddled with weaknesses and huge gaps in skills and abilities, and these gaps will never be filled unless somebody who thinks and feels differently is added to the team, which is why we now have diversity targets. The existence of diversity targets tells me that, at an intellectual level, we have figured out that there is a need for differences at the decision-making table, that we need diversity. However, if a person who is different does not feel respected and valued, she will quickly exit and find a group where she feels like she belongs. This is where inclusion enters the picture: the feeling of belonging and being respected and valued. Diversity targets will never be sustainably met without the creation of inclusive environments.

When you look at the teams in your life—your businesses, corporations, family—how easy is it for other people to show up just as they are? Do you have a culture that requires conformity, or do you have a culture that allows everyone to express their unique individualism? Do you celebrate differences or try to keep them quiet and shoved off to the side? Do you treat people as whole human beings with rich, deep lives, who care about things that really matter to them, or do you treat them like a number, a cog in the wheel, there only to produce one more widget in your factory?

Building a truly diverse and inclusive team culture in our companies or organizations starts with us as leaders. Are you holding yourself and your team accountable to be diverse and inclusive in your thinking, your hiring, your conversations that happen every day with every person you meet? What type of conversations do you tolerate, allow, and promote? Do you call out unwanted behavior and set an example for your team to follow? When you have a vacant position on your team, how much time do you spend thinking about what skill set is truly required to meet the needs of this role and what the team will benefit most from?

We cannot sit back and wait for the system to fix itself. We can all be the agents of change and the catalyst needed to get these wheels in motion. So, what are you doing today, this very minute, to make it different tomorrow?

We need to attract different people, including the mission-driven, minorities, and the socially-conscious Millennials who have ideas, perspectives, and experiences that are different from ours. We need to allow them to share their ideas and to challenge our way of thinking. We need to be open to trying something new so that we can push the boundaries of our current reality, heal the wrongs of the past generations, and move forward together.

We also need more role models. If you're a leader with visible minorities on your team, find them role models and mentors in senior positions with whom they can identify. If you are a senior leader of a visible minority, consider mentoring someone in your family, community, or corporation. If you're running your own business, reflect on how are you can pay it forward to someone just starting out. Challenge yourself to think about how to get more involved and make a bigger impact.

As parents, I believe it's our duty and responsibility to raise open-minded, inclusive children. I love the conversations we have around our dinner table in my home, where my kids challenge me on why I think the way I do and what I believe in. We are fortunate to live in a city where every person in my children's classroom looks different, thinks uniquely, and has different experiences. I find my children are not afraid to ask questions and are openly curious. Their questions come not from a place of exclusivity but, rather, come from a place of a genuine interest and a deep desire to understand. Even in families who might all look the same, there is diversity among us. My own children look like miniature versions of my husband and myself, yet they are so different from us and each other. Where one loves sports and being outdoors, the other wants to watch movies and craft. Where one always has a book on the go, the other would rather walk across hot coals than pick up the printed word. Food, clothing, and extracurricular activity preferences for each child are different—there is diversity in our own tiny family of five. In order to bring diversity into our working environments and our communities, we need to talk openly about our differences.

Can You Feel the Difference?

While we may not all be leaders, we are all part of a team, and as members of a team, we can feel the difference between an effective and ineffective leader immediately. As leaders, having the ability to quiet our minds, to slow down, and to take time for reflection, allows us to be able to tune into what our teams need from us. At the same time, we can also tune into what we need from ourselves. Grounded in this knowledge of what our team needs from us and what we need from ourselves, we can be effective leaders, equipped to set the vision, chart the course, and guide the ship.

Focusing solely on targets and numbers (the results portion of leadership) often leads to ineffective communication and disengagement of the team members. To illustrate this, I share a tale of two leaders whom I encountered while leading a technical group that supported two different regional teams.

The leader of one regional team (Team A)—we'll call him Pat—was one of the most effective leaders I've worked with. He was a proven leader in a different industry and came to our team excited, fresh, motivated, and inspiring. He didn't know anything about our business and had never heard of our company until he was recruited to join our team, but he was eager to learn and understand. Pat spent a great deal of time getting to know each and every one of us as team members, as individuals, and as contributors. We all felt valued and like an important part of his team. During meetings, our opinions were listened to, our experiences were valued, and our feedback was considered prior to moving forward. We were consulted during decisions regarding direction of our team members, their development plans, and their future goals.

During this same time, a new leader (Max) had just joined Team B. Max had worked his way up and was on track for senior management. Max's sales team members were feeling the wide range of emotions normally felt when leadership changes: optimism and excitement coupled with uncertainty and anxiety.

It was during Max's first team meeting that I began to notice how he completely changed the dynamics of what I considered a very veteran team. I noticed that many team members who were once open with their opinions were not speaking up. Opinions were not being shared and experiences were being ignored. We started out that day as a vibrant, connected team, challenging each other to grow the business, to push the boundaries, and to develop our people. As we shared our business overviews and current challenges, we were not met with consultative questions and curious inquiry from our new leader, Max. Instead, we were dismissed and scolded. We were talked down to and told "just do it this way." In short, we got to experience Max as the dictator in our very first interaction with him. When Team B walked away from that meeting room at the end of a very long day, they were a deflated, unmotivated, disconnected, and broken group of people, totally uninspired and beat down.

I had a long drive home after this meeting, and it was on that drive that I was able to reflect back on what just happened. About 45 minutes into my drive, my phone started ringing off the hook. I had critical and timely conversations with my peers and colleagues, who needed to connect and to know they had been seen and heard.

We had all just attended the meeting, and everyone was trying to sort through their emotions and rationalize their feelings based on what had just happened. No one was sure how to navigate the path going forward with Max. This team of high-performing individuals certainly didn't need a dictator type of leader telling them what to do every step of the way. From the team's point of view, Max had five minutes of experience in their business and with their customers; the existing team had decades of experience. It wasn't that they didn't want leadership. They were looking for a type of leadership that would honor their experience, their talents, and their ambition, and that would challenge them to look for new ways to increase sales, satisfy the customer, and develop their team.

By the time I got home, I had spent close to two hours talking to every single person that attended the meeting, and I heard the same thing from each person. No one was quite sure how they were going to make it through the next few years working for someone who led this way. I should say that in this organization, the moving around of leaders is fairly normal, so on the positive side, everyone knew that in a few years this person would likely be moved on. At the same time, the haunting questions remained: "How are we going to make it through the next few years until he's gone?" and "Can we survive?"

As the leader of the support team, I had no direct reporting line to Max. I made the decision to provide some feedback to him, because I genuinely believed he would not have acted the way that he acted, if he knew or understood the impact it had on the team. I gathered my notes with main talking points, which I find easier to write down before heading into somewhat difficult conversations. I reviewed the points I wanted to make and got Max on the phone. Looking back, I was a bit naïve.

While I didn't expect it, his defensive reaction was quite normal and something I should have anticipated. He couldn't believe what I was telling him. He honestly thought that there was nothing wrong with this behavior. We left the conversation without resolution. Half an hour later, Max called me back and proceeded to tell me that he had been in touch with every participant at the meeting, and informed me that nobody confirmed what I had told him, and that I must have been lying.

Now, do I hold it against the team members? Of course not. They reported directly to him and were stuck between a rock and a hard place when it came to confronting their new boss or staying quiet. They were trying to make the best of a bad situation. While it didn't surprise me that no one backed me up, I was disappointed. Change can only be brought about when we have the courage to speak about the injustices we see.

Max and I were unable to rebuild any sort of trust during the entire time he and I led together. I learned exactly what I didn't want to be. I remember to this day that experience of having a leader walk into a room and dismiss everything you said, and not acknowledge or even explore what you might know about the position or business you've dedicated yourself to for years. I vowed that I would do my best to remain consciously aware of the team members and always seek to understand their point of view, their challenges, and their strengths before offering coaching or direction to change.

Ineffective leadership feels like a coat that's too small. It's out of season, it's not in fashion, it's no longer stylish, and it doesn't feel good. You feel awkward. Your self-esteem is called into question, and your creativity suffers. You find yourself constantly adjusting, pulling at the coat, trying to smooth it out and make it feel okay, and yet, there is just something about it that is never quite right.

Effective leadership feels like your favorite pair of jeans, which are so comfortable and stylish that you could go anywhere in them without a second thought. When you have effective leadership, you don't have to hide parts of yourself; you can bring your whole self and be honored for the contribution you are making.

Making a decision to change leaders has a tremendous effect on the team. Changing one element in a team changes everything about the team. One person can bring about a shift in any group, team, or organization, and it happens almost immediately. My advice is to be aware, to stay present, and to understand that you will need to invest more time as a leader during times of change. This way, you can think through some of the impacts and better manage the emotions and fears as they arise.

I have a fundamental belief that change is for the better, even if we don't understand it at the time. Change provides learning opportunities and raises team effectiveness and productivity. New leadership should challenge us to grow in ways to better ourselves. It should not force us backward into old, unproductive behaviors and away from what we know to be true and authentic.

Who Do You Want to Be?

Leadership is about setting a direction, building a culture, and showing up with your whole self. It's about showing up as the person you want to be, with a clear passionate direction, standing firm in what will and will not be accepted from others. It's leadership, because people naturally want to follow you when you show up, representing yourself from a place of honesty, integrity, and vulnerability. We gravitate towards people who live their truths, who show their human side, and who have strong boundaries.

On one team I was a part of, the most senior engineer was promoted to a leadership position. He was the most obvious choice for someone to lead the team and none of us were surprised. About two years into his tenure, he stepped down from the role and assumed his senior engineering role again. I struggled to understand his decision at the time. How could he not want to be the leader? Wasn't that the point, to climb the ladder and get to the top? "Wow, did he ever miss the boat!" I thought. Clearly, I was still very early in my journey and just beginning to understand leadership.

About a year later, I was the one being promoted, and I became his leader. One of the first questions I had for him in our first meetings was why he left the role I was in now. Did he know something about the role that I didn't know yet? Was it a brutal job and no one was telling me? I was curious, to say the least.

His answered stunned me. He told me he stepped down because he realized that leading people wasn't his strength, and that he could be a bigger asset to our team as mentor and colleague rather than as our leader. He was a good engineer and loved solving complex problems for the clients we served, but he didn't at all enjoy leading a team of engineers.

He had taken the role knowing that it wasn't his passion nor his desired job, but felt the pressure to advance in the organization.

I look at this now and reflect on all my own experiences, where I've either been pushed into a role I didn't want or held back from one I really did want, and I realize how tragic this is. Organizations that follow rigid processes for advancement based on years in service, or years with the company, are missing a huge opportunity to maximize the effectiveness of their workforce, by overlooking more junior people who might have a natural strength for leadership. It's also tragic when we aren't sure of what we want. If we don't know what we want and where we want to go, then we don't know when to give an emphatic yes to a new opportunity, or when to respectfully decline.

If leaders of our organizations set clear expectations for what they need, not only for projects but also for positions, they are better able to seek out those who are best suited to fill those positions while maximizing team effectiveness. But it all starts with leaders knowing what they need and what their people want, and being able to find the synergies between the two.

CHAPTER 5:
CULTURE IS NOT A POSTER ON THE WALL

"Culture eats strategy for breakfast."
—Peter Druker, *Management consultant, Educator,*
and Author

In the last chapter, I talked about two different leaders, Max and Pat, who showed me the polar opposites of leadership. When leadership takes a direction that does not align with your own personal goals and values, you feel this change much sooner, than you'd feel the addition of someone who is aligned with your personally. I believe this to be true in most situations; we are quick to notice discomfort and things that aren't quite right and often take longer to notice comfort and the things we do like.

That feeling of "right" or "not right" is an indication of value alignment. All teams have a set of values, which are either written down or displayed as a poster on the wall, or sometimes just exist in unspoken form. These values serve as the foundation for the culture that is created. As a leader, you don't have to decide to set culture; it will happen regardless of your conscious or unconscious decision. If you want to be intentional, it will take work, dedication, and often tough decisions when it comes to your team. Leading a team is like parenting, and, like kids, the people in your organization will test the limits of your expectations and challenge you relentlessly on what behaviors and actions are acceptable.

Let's look at an example of a strong culture, one that is prevalent throughout the organization in all teams, regardless of function, department, or leader. I have only ever experienced this in one organization I've worked in, and I found it shocking. I was constantly surprised by the concentrated efforts and the focus required to maintain this culture. I remember thinking during my first days of culture training (yes, there was culture training), "Wow, if this is actually how the company is run, I can't wait to get started! But I'm pretty sure this is a one-time thing, and once I get back to my team, I'll have to get to know my leader and how he wants things done."

I couldn't have been more wrong. Every year, everyone in the company spent an average of two days on culture training. Now, we weren't all robots, stripped of all free will and independent thought. Quite the opposite actually happened. We were given clear rules of engagement, clear expectations, clear goals, and a framework for development. This allowed me to experience a freedom I had never felt before, the freedom to achieve my goals in a way that I found personally satisfying and the freedom to work in a way which supported my life. I knew how to engage in conversations with other team members, regardless of who their leader was. In short, we had a common language and a common set of behaviors across the company, not just in our team, but across a company that is present in 120 countries and has over 20,000 employees worldwide. This astounds me.

On the other hand, I have also experienced the exact opposite. I have worked for both a small, family-owned company with local employees and a publicly traded organization with global presence, where there was no common corporate leadership language or rules of engagement. Depending on who you were working for and what project you were on, you could expect very different acceptable behaviors, management efforts, and developmental support. This was the "who you know" culture and the values in those companies were just posters on the wall, hardly even worth the paper they were printed on. People acted in contradiction to these printed articles constantly, and not only did no one say a word, but nothing was done about this conflicting behavior.

If the culture set by leadership can be so easily felt by team members and so drastically different, how does culture actually come about? Call me an idealist or maybe even a little naïve, but I truly believe that there is a way to build this type of culture and system, one that provides support that is both rigid enough to hold people and keep them focused on the common goals, while flexible enough to allow them to find their space and their own way to work within the bigger system.

Most people become disengaged when they can't see how their work directly contributes to the overall good of the company. I have experienced this as an employee and have coached team members through these types of situations. Most of us inherently have a desire to do meaningful, worthwhile work, so when we can't see how our work ties in to the greater good of the organization or the team that we work for, it's hard to stay engaged in it, or to believe that it's meaningful or worthwhile.

Do your people know their work is worthwhile, and know how it translates and directly ties into where the company is going? Do they know why they're doing the tasks you've asked them to do? Do you know why you're doing the things that you're doing as a business owner, entrepreneur, or team leader? If you don't know why you're doing what you're doing, it's difficult imagine that your team knows why they're doing what they're doing.

One of my favorite reads on this topic is the book *Gung Ho* by Ken Blanchard. Blanchard talks about three principles that are required for any group of people, team, or organization to develop true effectiveness, high productivity, and open communication.

The first principle is analogous to the spirit of the squirrel, who devotes his life to simple, worthwhile work. Squirrels gather nuts for the winter and store them away. This gathering and storing of food directly connects to survival. Every squirrel knows this, and the more each squirrel puts away for the winter, the better their chance of survival. Does your team know what their most critical tasks are, how those tasks tie back into the organization, and why they're important? Can they clearly articulate what it is they do, and why it's worthwhile and meaningful for the company? The answer should be a clear and resounding "yes." If it's not, you have work to do as their leader to define and explain what it is they do that is meaningful and worthwhile, not only to your team and organization, but also to themselves.

The next principle is called the way of the beaver, which represents control of achieving the goal. Blanchard talks about how the beaver knows that the dam has to be built and how to build it (worthwhile work); however, every beaver is free to go about cutting different size trees, from different places, hauling them back to the damn. Not one beaver does this the same way, but the damn gets built and they have a home to live in. Often, this fundamental principle of autonomy, to get the job done how I need to get the job done, is missing in teams. Most often, the team operates with a leadership style that is more like "do it my way, because I'm the leader, and I think it should be done this way." It's a subtle distinction, but it usually means the difference between high employee engagement and total disengagement, where team members come to work just to punch a clock. Do you have this type of culture in your team? How freely are the people in your organization, team, or company able to do work in a way that suits them best, and allows for the maximum productivity that they can achieve?

The third principle is called the gift of the goose and speaks to cheering each other on. When a flock of geese flies overhead, you hear them often before you see them; their sounds are almost deafening. And if you watch closely, you'll see that quite often the bird in the lead, the one at the very tip of the "V," will only lead for a short period of time and slowly it will move back and find its way to the tail end of the "V," with a new bird moving forward to lead the flock. The honking is the sound of the geese cheering each other on as they all take turns at the lead. How often do you celebrate success on your team? Do you have an employee recognition reward system in your company, business, or team? Even just a simple thank you card goes a long way to showing people that they are valued and recognized.

Work That Matters

How many of you have had goals given to you by your manager that you didn't understand, that the manager couldn't explain, and that you ultimately had no control over? For me, this has happened far too often. Having a goal given to me that I don't understand, and that I have no control over, is demotivating and disengaging. And, naturally, I find it challenging to look up to leaders who can't explain why a goal is important and how my success contributes to the success of the team.

Your team needs to know that their work makes a difference and that it matters. This knowledge is fundamental to success. And knowing that the work you're doing as the leader is important, is fundamental to your commitment to getting the job done. Imagine if you started working at a business and were just told to run it. And imagine if you didn't know what work the team you were just made the leader of actually did, and were just told to lead them. Sounds ridiculous, doesn't it? And, yet, this is often what happens when we dictate company goals and targets to working team members.

Impersonal goals never work. Ever. If we don't know why we are doing what we've been asked to do, if we cannot see the task's importance, and if the difference our work will make is not clear to us, we simply won't do it. Many may start the task and some might finish, but no one will ever execute the undefined work to the best of their abilities.

Imagine if I said to you, "I need a business case for XYZ product by Monday." If we have a history and you've done this before for me, you have a fairly high chance of actually completing this task to my liking. However, if you are new to my team or if you've never done this type of task before, you will likely become completely frustrated during the completion of this report. It would probably end up looking something like this:

Week 1 - You spend time doing company and Google research for samples and examples of good business reports. At the end of the week, I ask how you are doing and if we can review a draft by Monday.

Weekend 1 - You spend the entire weekend working, freaking out because you had no idea that report was required so quickly. Feelings of self-doubt creep in. You doubt your worthiness and competence to even stay in this role and quickly become overwhelmed. You might be able to produce something for Monday; it definitely will not be your best work, but it will suffice. Or, you might retreat and give up, maybe call in sick on Monday to try and buy a bit more time.

Week 2 - We meet to discuss the report. You've shown up with a 15-page, fairly comprehensive document, and I am a bit shocked, as I was looking for a rough outline, table of contents, and ZERO content. You are now furious that you gave up the concert tickets, missed your daughter's soccer game, and ate take out all weekend, killing yourself to develop the draft report. I now understand why it took so long to get to this place, and perhaps, even brush off all the time you've invested thus far. We review the table of contents and rough organization of the report, I make some changes and suggestions, and you leave with the task of completing the report based on this new outline in two weeks.

Weeks 3 and 4 - You furiously work away at research: market trends, consumer data, political environment, you name it, you're including it in your report. After all, you love this type of thing. I stop by a few times during this two-week period to ask how you are doing and if everything is going well. You note that things are on track and all is good.

Week 5 - Final copy is delivered to me in a 3-inch binder, which weighs approximately ten pounds. You are so proud of all of your hard work, all of the research, all the comparative notes; this is one of your best products so far in your career. I, on the other hand, am appalled and wondering how in the world we ended up this far apart on our expectations of what this report should look like. It's so simple! This thing that was delivered is too big, and there is simply way too much information in this report.

Week 6 - I find a more seasoned person on the team to revamp the report, someone who has done this a million times before and knows exactly what is needed. By the end of the week, there is a concise report ready to go. You have found out through the office grapevine that someone else is making edits on your report. You feel hurt and frustrated. No one has spoken to you regarding the report, and, as far as you know, it was a quality piece of work that you were proud of. You are left feeling disengaged and believing that your work is not valued by me and perhaps not by the entire organization.

If we dissect the situation above, we will find the root cause is likely that the team member didn't know why the business case was important, and that the leader took no time to explain how the team member's contribution of completing the business case would impact the company's success.

People can't succeed at the what, the specific task, action, or behavior, if they don't understand the why, the significance of that specific task, action, or behavior. Once you've identified and confirmed that the team member understands why that specific work is important and necessary to the company, you will need to land on fairly specific goals and actions that you and the team member agree upon.

This is where a lot of people will talk about S.M.A.R.T. goals. S.M.A.R.T stands for Specific, Measurable, Attainable, Relevant and Time bound, or some variation thereof. Even though I'm a fan, I don't think they are the be-all and end-all of goal setting. The most important, critical and often over-looked step in setting a goal is outlining the steps to achieving that goal.

In cases where the team member can't directly complete the goal, such as company or team goals, it will be the team member's actions that will be critical to nail down. They have direct control over their actions, and you will be able to track, monitor, and correct behaviors depending on the outcome achieved.

Being in Control

So, now that we know why the work is important and what needs to be done to achieve the goals, it's time to get to work, right? Wait, you want me to be in the office from 8am until 5pm every day, with only a 30-minute lunch break? This is so not what I signed up for!

Enter into the world of control, specifically being in control of the goal. I mean, who doesn't like to be control? We all, to varying degrees, like to have control of our time. With the changing technology and virtual work environments, gone are the days where we all have to be tied to our desks in a physical office location to get the work done. Today, you don't have to even be on the same continent to attend a board meeting. (Granted, there are still some professions which do require to you to be in a physical location for a specific amount of time, but the person who thrives in that environment probably isn't reading this book. If you are currently in a position that demands showing up physically for a specified time and you don't like it, it's time to think about making a change, my friend.)

So, when it comes to getting those big goals and actions done, crossing off the to-do list and hitting those targets, one of the best ways to empower your team to perform is to let them have some control over how they get them done. Notice I said "some" control here. Not all the control.

Giving control can take on many different forms, depending on your business and your company's pre-existing culture.

Find out where to you have some flexibility, identify what boundaries you could push, and then go from there. You must have clearly defined actions and/or deliverables that can be measured, for a more flexible work environment to work effectively. If you spend the time up-front, being clear about what you need and defining success, allowing team members to choose how they work can be one of the most engaging and motivating gifts you give your team.

Some ideas for flexible work schedules that give team members control include:

1. Working from home mornings or afternoons, or one or two days per week.

2. Working a compressed work week (e.g., four to ten hours per day versus five to eight hours per day).

3. Flexible work hours with a core time to be present (e.g., team members must be available from 10 am to 2 pm on specific days of the week, and the rest of the hours they work as it suits them).

4. Allowing team members to change the scripted message to one that sounds more personal and genuine while maintaining the core message.

5. Providing a budget for training with an approval process that doesn't mandate everyone taking the same course delivered in the same way. We all learn differently; support the learning and let go of the delivery method.

6. Part-time positions, or hiring two part time people to fill one full-time role, a form of job-sharing, work well for some positions and could be explored if suitable.

The second part of making all of this work is providing the team with expectations – not rules. I call these Expectations of Engagement, and they're basic guidelines written down to help the team work effectively together. Be careful to not fall into the trap of thinking, "These are so common sense—I can't believe we had to write these down!" They are only common sense if everyone on your team thinks and acts like you and shares the same perspectives, beliefs, and values. Even if the only difference on your team is male and female or 20-year-olds and 40-year-olds, that's enough diversity to require that you write down how you as the leader expect everyone to work together.

Expectations of Engagement might look like this:

1. We will ask curious questions first to explore and confirm our understanding.

2. We will act with integrity in all we do and respect our differences.

3. We will collaborate to bring out the best ideas and increase innovation.

4. We will celebrate each other by (insert team recognition program here).

5. We will have FUN in all we do.

This is just a starting point. The expectations of engagement will be different for every organization, company, and team.

The more defined the goals, actions, and behaviors are in your team, the more control you can relinquish on how the work gets done. If you spend your time as the leader monitoring the goal completion and enforcing the Expectations of Engagement, you won't have to spend a lot time worrying about how the work gets done. The results will speak for themselves.

Celebrate!

If you're reading the book, I'm going to assume that you work hard. We live in a time where people are more overworked and stressed-out than at any other point in modern history, contributing to record rates of physical and mental illness. I think it's time we had more time for celebration and more time to connect with the people with whom we spend the better part of our days.

Celebrating each other at work doesn't need to be grand or flashy, nor does it require a big investment of time or money. To be successful, all that is required is an honest intention and some creative thoughtfulness. A simple thank you card is enough to brighten someone's day and make them feel like their work matters.

I've had experience with no recognition, to the point I often wondered if it even mattered if I showed up at work, and the complete opposite end of the spectrum where the praise and accolades felt uncomfortably over the top. I'm aiming for the sweet spot in the middle, where the recognition and celebrations feel worthy and appropriate, where each team member can feel that that they are seen and that their contribution is valued.

Recognition, celebration, team building, party time—whatever you want to call it, it can take on various forms, a few of which I've outlined below to get you thinking about some possibilities for your team.

1. Give every team 10 thank you cards to be used by the end of the calendar year with their teammates or others in the company.

2. Work with the other leaders and/or the company social club to provide tickets to movies, events, etc., which can be purchased at a discount and shared with someone who went above and beyond.

3. Plan a team building event and go as big as the budget allows, whether it's an afternoon of paintball, a potluck once a month, a bake sale, a group exercise class, or a three-day, offsite retreat.

4. Have some $5 gift cards on hand to the local coffee shop, tea house, or lunch spot and hand them out the day after everyone pulls an all-nighter meeting for a huge deadline or launch date.

5. Take the team out for lunch or Friday afternoon beverages. Unexpected events work well to boost morale and are often better attended than events planned in advance.

Hopefully this list gets the ideas flowing and provides some inspiration for you to take action. If you lead a team, you need to show them that having fun and celebrating each other are important. For this to work, you need to lead by example and stay out in front!

CHAPTER 6: EXPLORING EXPECTATIONS

"Expectations are resentments under construction."
—Anne Lamott, *Author, Public Speaker, Activist*

Uncommunicated expectations are the silent killer of effective teams and relationships.

Picture a speed bump—you know, the kind they put in residential areas for traffic-calming purposes. I've lived in many neighborhoods that, over the years, have had speed bumps added. The first time we hit the new speed bump in our neighborhood, probably going a little too fast, we send everyone who's in the car with us ricocheting around.

Once we realize the speed bump is there, we slow down. Expectations are this speed bump, and this is exactly what happens when we have expectations of people that they are unaware of. Unspoken expectations are just like that new speed bump we didn't know was there. Once we communicate our expectations, we can more easily navigate around or over them, barely feeling the impact.

I have been driving over expectation speed bumps my entire life. The times I am able to navigate these speed bumps are the times when I'm in tune with my own strengths and skills in the situation, and have effectively communicated my expectations. During these times of successful navigation, I've noticed that my expectations of others are also much more aligned with their skills, strengths, and capabilities. I've spent time working to understand and reflect on what I'm expecting of the team member, versus what they are capable of at their given stage of development.

Expectations of Others

Let's go back to our example of the business case preparation from Chapter 5. My expectations of my team member created a huge speed bump in our relationship; I expected that they knew what to do, and I expected that they would come ask for help if they were unsure of what to do. I didn't not communicate this, nor did I confirm understanding.

expectations + no communication = huge speed bump →
resentment, disappointment, misalignment

(By the way, this is common to all relationships, not just
those at the office!)

Most people show up wanting to give their best, and very few
people are comfortable with saying "I don't know how to do
that. Would you help me learn?" or "I'm not clear on what
you're asking me to do. Would you explain it in a different
way?" because they fear being seen as incompetent or unable
to handle the job. Leading with empathy and creating an
inclusive environment means that, as leaders, we create space
for these questions to be asked. We encourage people to ask
for help, to seek out new and different perspectives, and to
know that we support learning at all levels. These simple
questions are very powerful tools that are highly effective at
minimizing expectation speed bumps.

It's critical we spend time getting to know and understand
our team members. We need to know their current strengths,
skills, and capabilities, and we need to have a vision for them
to grow in to. In my pervious example of the business case,
a lot of frustration could have been avoided and a lot of
time better utilized, if I had initiated a conversation with my
team member. The conversation should have been focused
on understanding my team member's skills and abilities,

and clearly outlining my expectations of the assignment. Two outcomes are possible here: either the assignment was a fit for this team member and they would have gone on to execute it with a desirable outcome, or I would have found out that this assignment wasn't right for this employee right now and would have assigned it to a different team member. Either way would be a much better use of everyone's time, talents, and resources.

Expectations of Yourself

We don't just have expectations of other people; we also have expectations of ourselves, and the end result of resentment, disappointment, and misalignment still hold true. Here's an example of a recent inner dialogue:

[Me] "Ugh, I just can't ever seem to get everything I want to do in a day done!"

[Inner Critic] *"Why can't you be better at planning?"*

[Me] "I'm a project manager, and people pay me to be organized and get things done. Why do I struggle so much in my personal life?"

[Inner Critic] *"What was your 'to-do' list today? Did you even make one?"*

[Me] "Well, I thought I wanted to cook the family a nice breakfast, clean up the house, catch up on the laundry, get some gardening done, and I would like to sit down and read for an hour. I also really need to catch up with my dear friend, so I've invited her family over at 4 pm for drinks and dinner. The kids need to finish their homework, and Henry needs me to help him out on that school project. At the end of the day I would love to wind down in a hot bath and soak the day away. Oh, and I really need to get that 5 km training run in today as well!"

[Inner Critic] "Really? You wanted to get all that done in one day? Why can't you ever say no?!"

[Me] "Ya, I thought I could. I'm just not going to, and I'm really frustrated with myself for being so lazy!"

Any of this sounding vaguely familiar? I often have this type of conversation with myself; the content varies, but it always centers on what I thought I could get done, and what I was actually able to do. It's all about the expectations I have of myself. The best way I've found to bring awareness and overcome this frustration is to, first, catch myself in this conversation cycle and take a deep breath, and, second, ask myself, "What would you tell a close friend if they came to you with this?"

As a result of consistent practice, I've been catching myself earlier in the conversation; the conversation hasn't stopped and the voice in my head is still there (and some days very overactive), but I have learned to interrupt the chatter sooner, which leads to a very different outcome than before. I can now offer myself compassion and understanding that wasn't always available to me. I am better as recognizing my own emotions in a situation and not becoming defensive, which allows me to hold space for, see, and hear everyone in the conversation.

We have a compassion for others that we don't often apply to ourselves. For some reason, it's okay for someone else to take a break, hire a housekeeper, order take out, sit down and read, and go for the run. But when it comes to ourselves, we self-impose an all-or-nothing approach. Now, maybe you already have this self-compassion super power, and, if you do, I applaud you. It's a gift that many people strive to build most of their lives. For the rest of us, this simple exercise can be implemented anytime, anywhere, and will help you start to develop self-compassion and be able to set realistic expectations for yourself.

We often place the bar for ourselves where we expect others to perform, usually unconsciously and unintentionally. We default to a place that applies the logic, that if I can do it, anyone can. Understanding and gaining awareness of the expectations we place on ourselves, allows us to separate our expectations for ourselves versus those of our team members. When you start to see the expectation speed bumps around you, you will automatically be able to be more compassionate and less frustrated with yourself and with your team.

People will either rise to the challenge placed in front of them or they will shrink to the mediocrity that is tolerated. So, do you expect the best from people or do you tolerate average? Spend time getting to know your team member and their strengths and passions, so that you can make the most of those qualities and can support that individual in reaching their full potential. And spend some time getting to know yourself. Commit to a lifetime of learning and growing, and setting appropriate expectations accordingly, sharing them out loud with those around you to navigate those speed bumps together as a team.

Start Where You Are

While the journey for me began when I was child, knowing and trusting myself as a leader developed when I started spending time getting to know and understand my true self. One of my biggest awakenings was in learning to understand and leverage my empathy. As I mentioned earlier, my empathy used to manifest as being overly emotional and unstable, with regular crying breakdowns in my leaders' offices. It was embarrassing, and for years, I tried to do what everyone asked. Get your emotions under control. Learn to toughen up. Put on your game face. Never let them see you cry.

For 10 years, I tried and tried but I could never master any of these things. I became frustrated with myself. The more time that passed, the more I detested this emotional side of myself. I started thinking that I wasn't cut out for leadership, even though I really enjoyed the work I did, the conversations I had, and the personal connections I made. In some moments, I could be effective and feel like I was making a difference, and then, in the next moment, I would be an emotional wreck, convinced that I just couldn't hack it. How could I be so effective at leading people, except when it came to tough conversations or difficult situations? Why did I turn into this wreck who couldn't seem to pull herself together?

In 2010, one of my leaders recommended Tim Rath's *Strength Finders 2.0*, a book that helps people assess their strengths. I bought the book in an airport bookstore on one of my many work trips, and it travelled between the corner of my desk and nightstand for months (I moved it around, thinking that I would get to it sooner). At this point, I had three kids under the age of seven, and my husband and I both had full-time careers. If I was reading anything, it wasn't for self-development; it was to escape the daily grind, to turn off my brain, and to retreat into some fantasy world for just a few moments, in hopes of maintaining my sanity.

One day, I put the *Strengths Finder* book into my backpack and took the assessment test while sitting in an airport, waiting for a flight. I will never forget that day. It was the day I learned that my empathy may not be a weakness, and was not something I need to fix. Rather, it was one of my greatest strengths and should be leveraged as it was rare, coveted, and necessary to leading effectively. What?! Necessary to leading effectively, really? I wasn't yet convinced, so I spent the rest of my trip reading and re-reading my assessment results.

Here is an excerpt from the results:

People with strong Empathy talents can sense the emotions of those around them. They can feel what others are feeling as though the emotions were their own. They intuitively see the world through others' eyes and share their perspectives. They perceive people's pain or joy—sometimes before it is even expressed. Their instinctive ability to understand is powerful. They can hear unvoiced questions and anticipate needs. Where others grapple for words, they seem to find the right things to say and strike the right tone. As a result, they help people express their feelings—to themselves as well as to others. They help people give voice to their emotional lives.

"They feel what others are feeling as though the emotions were their own." Could this be why I would end up so overwhelmed and stressed out when things at work were tense? Was I picking up on everyone else's emotions? Maybe my outbursts and inability to handle my emotions weren't really problems after all. I just couldn't handle a whole office or team full of emotions without understanding what I was dealing with.

This revelation changed my life. Instead of working to pour all of my energy and resources trying to fix my emotional self, I could now focus on recognizing my emotions and my team members' emotions, so that I could help everyone understand their feelings and express them effectively. Doing this would assist the team in navigating turbulent and changing times.

I began to embrace my empathy, and to use it in the teams I was a part of, and in the teams I was leading. I also helped other leaders who didn't have this strength to understand their own teams. Once I became adept at leveraging this skill, leaders from all levels of the organization came to me for the "temperature" of the teams on a regular basis, especially during times of change, reorganization, and upheaval. It was liberating.

For those of you who are curious, my strengths as defined by *Strength Finders* are: Responsibility, Empathy, Developer,

110

Belief, and Discipline. I truly identify with these strengths, and the awareness that has been gained in knowing and understanding all aspects of my strengths has made me a more effective leader, both personally and professionally. As with all good things, when used in excess, they can become weaknesses or blind spots; it's all about harmony. Regular self-checks and ongoing review are essential in my own development and growth, to ensure that I remain open to feedback and adjust with my team, my environment, and my situation.

Spend some time getting to know yourself in whatever way feels right for you.

"Getting to know yourself" happens when you are curious and ask open ended questions like:

- *What are my dreams?*

- *How do I want to feel?*

- *What do I love to do?*

- *What do I know I never want to do again?*

You can also complete any or all of the following:

- Assessments, both free or paid, in-person or online (see the Resources section for a few suggestions)

- Coaching, either one-on-one or in a group

- Therapy

- Meditation and reflection

- Yoga

- Asking friends and family (this is a Pandora's box of feedback, so be warned!)

- Floating (more on this in Chapter 12)

- Reading self-development and self-help books (see the Resources section for a few suggestions)

Once you have gathered the data from whatever source you deemed appropriate, spend some time with it. Be curious and explore what you have in front of you. What fits? What doesn't? What have people been telling you that you do well? Do you identify with this? What are your perceived weaknesses? Are they actually weaknesses or just a misunderstood and underutilized strength? Enter a phase of researching and understanding yourself. You may be surprised by what you find.

Getting to truly know yourself is scary, messy, and hard work. Separating who we think we are, and who our loved ones think we are, from the real self that is usually buried deep inside is difficult, but self-discovery is an essential element to successful, authentic, and true leadership. The journey of self-discovery is one that we must commit to for a lifetime, so that we are constantly curious and asking questions as part of the never-ending search to understand ourselves. Through understanding ourselves, we develop compassion and a capacity for tolerance, appreciation, and genuine acceptance of those who differ from us. It is through this journey we become not only leaders of diverse teams but champions of inclusion.

CHAPTER 7 : DEFEATING DAMAGING MYTHS

"When you change the way you look at things, the things you look at change."
—Wayne Dyer, *Author, Speaker, Philosopher*

Experience Equals Gray Hair

Myth: To be a leader you need years of experience, multiple degrees, and a whole lot of gray hair.

Reality: Leadership requires an ability to listen to and connect with the people you lead, regardless of degrees earned or prior experience.

I have been formally in a leadership role for a decade, I don't have an MBA, and I color my gray hair. I am an empath, and I've been informally leading my entire life. My leadership degree is from the school of real life, and my experience is vast and varied. I am who I am, and you are who you are; there is no standard formula for what it means to be a leader, and the types of leadership are as varied and unique as the types of individuals who lead.

However, there are skills that you can develop and hone over your lifetime of leadership. While there are many schools of thoughts and entire sections of the bookstore filled with ideas on where to start, I believe you are best rewarded as a leader if you narrow your focus to just two skills to start with. Two foundational skills sets include the skill of listening with the intention to understand, not respond and the skill of connecting with the whole person whom you are leading. If more leaders worked on honing these two skills, our workplaces and teams would look and feel very different, than what we experience currently in most corporate cultures.

I can hear you already, thinking, "What about technical competencies, experience, and knowledge? Aren't those skills important, too?"

If I have excellent abilities when it comes to listening to people and making connections, would it not stand to reason that my experiences will be deeper, richer, and more fulfilling? That I would be open to constructive feedback regarding my skills and abilities, and would be more likely to hear the message, actively address the feedback, and work to improve myself so that those who interact with me have a more positive experience? That I would be able to create higher performing teams faster than someone who wasn't as skilled in these areas?

Ultimately, increasing the value of experiences and increasing engagement, contributes to building high performing teams. With enhanced engagement, people would be responsible for work that they were passionate about, and team members would come to know and feel safe in bringing their whole selves to work, which allows for deeper connections and more authentic experiences. With active listening, seeking to understand and connect with people automatically provides opportunities to enhance competencies, experiences, and knowledge.

Let me share with you a story of a magnetic woman whom I had the chance to lead, to demonstrate the power of listening and connection, two skills that not only help build effective teams, but also help build effective lives.

I first met Ruth when we worked on a committee together. She was a go-getter, driven and high-achieving. She presented herself to me, and to others, as someone who knew her path, what she wanted, and how she was going to get it, and she was steadfast in her vision of her career.

I had an opening on my team and was seeking someone who was driven and had the ability to take complex issues and make them into simple processes. Ruth came to me and asked about the position, even though she wasn't crazy about getting into project work. As an HR professional, she wasn't sure that this was the right move for her career-wise, but she wanted to work with me. My first reaction was feeling flattered, and then fear and doubt settled in. I questioned my ability to lead this powerful force of a woman and I feared being found out a fraud, threatened almost immediately by her presence.

Ruth applied, and she had the credentials to get an interview, so my director and I sat down with her. She blew us both away. Ruth joined my team, and we began our journey together. I spent five months as Ruth's direct leader. During our first few months together, we were learning about each other: what support she required, how we communicated together, where we aligned or where we had gaps. Things were going really well. I finally had my dream team. But our time together was limited; I was moved to a different team shortly after Ruth came on board.

Ruth was upset that I was moving teams. She felt let down by the organization, as she had moved out of the HR stream specifically to work with me. She didn't want to stay if she couldn't work with me. As I was leaving my team, I told her that we could continue to meet monthly for mentoring sessions and stay connected, so that we could continue our growth and development together.

Moving to my new role was a rollercoaster for me. Thrown off the deep end with no support, I inherited a team full of unmotivated and dissenting people, and a project that was highly controversial. However, I vowed to keep my commitment to Ruth through this time, and we began meeting monthly. Our meetings ended up being a highlight for me during this time. I believe that the quality of our relationship was born out of my ability to listen to her experiences, reflect back what I was hearing, and help her see what she couldn't see. Sometimes, insights came out of a story of my own experience, or sometimes just through talking the situation through together. Our biggest connection was actually our shared journey as mothers.

About a year and a half after I met Ruth, my daughter Olivia was diagnosed with learning disabilities and ADHD (attention deficit/hyperactivity disorder) after a four-year-long academic struggle. It was a very hard time for me. I was filled with blame, guilt, and feelings of shame that I initially didn't understand, nor did I feel like I had the time to explore. Action needed to be taken. In one of our monthly mentoring sessions, I was visibly upset, and so I shared what was going on in my personal life with Ruth. I was stunned at the compassion and connection that happened in that moment. Even though she had children younger than mine, Ruth could completely identify with my story, as one of her daughters was also struggling in school, and she couldn't figure out what the source of the problem was. In sharing my story, she saw glimpses of herself and her daughter, and it moved her to start asking different questions and taking action toward a resolution.

At this point in my own journey, I decided to take a leave from my corporate career to be at home with my children and support them through this transition. Our daughter needed a lot of remediation tutoring and special programming, which took a lot of my time, and I also wanted to have time for my sons. I didn't see how I could work 50-60 hours a week and still have time for the children, my marriage, and myself. I remember telling Ruth, and she was quite stunned at first, and then very inquisitive about my decision to put my career on hold. Her probing made me question my decision for a few minutes, but, in the end, I knew I had to follow my instincts and trust that everything would work out.

Ruth and I have remained in touch since I left the corporate world, and it was during our last meeting together that I got a true sense of the impact our relationship has had on her life. She told me that she had begun exploring her own career decisions, goals, and aspirations after watching me make this radical change in my life. She met with her daughter's teachers and is getting assessment work pushed forward, realizing that the work she does in this world matters more than the paycheck. She realized just how much of her soul she was being denied by putting the paycheck ahead of her daily experience, and the status of a title ahead of the impact of her work.

Ruth is now actively pursuing a career change, focused on making a positive impact in the world, feeding her passions, and listening to her soul. She wants to have time to spend with her children and husband, and time to enjoy her own hobbies and passions outside the office. I believe that it was through my ability to make a deep, meaningful connection with this wonderful woman and to truly listen to what she had to say, that together we were able to both stand in our own truths, become leaders of our lives, and avoid falling victim to our circumstances. Rather, we were both able to rise above our current situations, define and chart a new course, and move boldly toward our visions.

I don't have 30 years of experience, an advanced degree, or too much gray hair (yet!), but I can lead. I do have valuable experience, and I am capable.

Shattering the Glass Ceiling

Myth: The glass ceiling has kept me from advancing in my career.

Reality: You will never shatter the glass ceiling if you can't get your feet off the sticky floor.

The more time I spend in my career, the more opportunities I have to talk to mid-career women. I'm finding that more and more I am faced with the reality that we will move in and out of organizations—to raise our children, to care for family members, to maintain our health - and there is uncertainty by management as to what to do with us when this movement occurs. Is it worth investing in us, even though we might choose to stay at home permanently? Can they trust us to come back? How will it be perceived if they promote someone who has just taken time off? I'm going to venture that regardless of the length of your leave, or the reason for it, we all face very similar realities when returning to our careers.

When I was a little girl, I heard all kinds of talk of the glass ceiling. Once I knew what it was, I became convinced that it didn't apply to me, or that I would just smash it to pieces. Currently, the reality is that I'm still trying to reach the ceiling, which keeps feeling farther and farther away.

And perhaps it is moving farther away, because of the phenomenon women of my generation face: the sticky floor. The sticky floor metaphor is used to describe situations where women somehow hold themselves back, either consciously or unconsciously. The metaphors of sticky floors and glass ceilings resonate deeply with me. I have felt for my entire career that there is no shortage of women who want to have a rewarding, fulfilling, exciting, high-level career. They have the skills to match their male counterparts and a desire to reach the top. Yet, most of us are still unable to reach the heights we desire. I have certainly felt stuck in a system that's broken and not built to meet our unique and specific individual needs. And I needed a wakeup call to get me out of a victim mindset, which leads us to the sticky floor.

Now, it wasn't easy to think that I may have been holding myself back. I didn't want to face this reality at first, and it was a hard part of myself to look at. It won't be easy for you to do this work either, but that's okay; not being easy is not the same as not being achievable.

Yes, there are systemic issues in organizations creating barriers, but, at the same time, there are real, tangible situations in which we hold ourselves back and devalue ourselves. In order to shatter that glass ceiling, we must be able to pick our feet up from the sticky floor. And to be able to do that, we have to stop blaming others, stop looking outside ourselves, and recognize that we hold keys to both.

Start by asking for what you want, clearly and concisely. If you want to be vice president on the board of directors or own your own company, declare it. It doesn't mean it will happen right away, but asking for it out loud and letting your desire be known will make it possible for others to help you get there.

Kick out the perfectionist inside of you. You know who I mean—she lives there, deep inside you, and likes to run the show. She does not serve you in getting off the floor or in shattering the ceiling. The quicker you can embrace your faults and own your imperfections, the more likely you are to put your work forward, become visible, and engage in the conversation going on around you.

Embrace and practice empathy. (As you may have realized, empathy is kind of my thing.) Empathy allows us to connect with others, to build a support network, and opens up greater access to our own feelings and the feelings of others. This helps us to navigate potentially political situations with ease and gives us the voice to speak up with genuine intent, instead of waiting for the right place and right time. Empathy also helps us navigate challenges in finding the harmony between our personal and professional obligations. Practicing empathy shows us that asking for help is a sign of strength, not weakness, and that we can all support each other to reach the top, where we all deserve to be, whatever the top may look like for each of us.

Asking for what you want, dropping the mask of perfectionism, and practicing empathy will allow you to been seen, be heard, and be in control of your future. Your feet will come off the sticky floor, and you'll be headed straight for the glass ceiling. I can't wait to see it shatter!

Defining Success

Myth: To succeed in a man's world, act like a man.

Reality: You don't need to compromise yourself or try to fit into someone else's mold; the world needs what you have to offer.

Almost every female senior leader I've heard speak over the past 15 years, has delivered some variation of the message that, in order to succeed in the man's world, we women need to act and think like men. It's the old "if you can't beat 'em, join 'em" mentality. Quite frankly, I'm tired of it, and I don't buy into it. I am not a man, I don't think like a man, and I don't act like a man.

Some of the messages I've heard from other female leaders include:

> "I'm single. I don't have time for a relationship."
> "I'm married but don't have kids."
> "I have kids, and my partner stays home."

The basic message boils down to, if you are from a dual-working-parent family with kids, don't even think about making it to the top. And if that's true, just come out and tell me, so I can quit banging my head against walls and ceilings in organizations I'll never succeed in. But it's not true. I'm told I can do more and perform better than most above me, and, yet, I feel stuck on the floor of a system that I can't see a way out of. In experiencing this, I realized that if I stayed and accepted this as just the way it is, it will not change for me or my children. And I want this system to change for my sons and my daughter.

But, do I stay or do I go? Changing corporate culture is like changing the course of the Titanic. Can it be done in time or will we hit the iceberg? Are you the first one on the lifeboat, or do you go down with the ship?

I'm married, and I would like to stay that way. I like to work, and so does my husband. We have children. These are things about my life I am not prepared to change. So how do I find an environment in which I thrive? How do I do meaningful work in the world? How do I make my contribution?

I have to tell my story, and I don't have to accept that what's been in the past is what should be done in the future. I don't think anyone is asking for a complete 180-degree shift; rather, we need to see steady movement, 10 or 20 degrees at a time.

But how to do that?

- Tell our stories and be pleasantly persistent about sharing our real experiences.

- Be courageous, and if you can't change the situation, change your situation.

- Stop telling younger generations what we've experienced is what they should expect to experience.

- Recognize that my way doesn't equal your way.

I think of the women who fought for our right to vote, to attend school and get an education, to participate in politics, and to become doctors, engineers, police officers, and pilots. I think of all of the men who are primary caregivers to their kids, who make dinner, provide taxi services to events, and plan birthday parties. And I think of all the families like mine who have two working parents, who both want to participate in their kids' lives. I think of all the people who don't want to be entrepreneurs, and of the entrepreneurs who have thriving businesses in need of a team. We all enjoy having the security that's comes with what our work provides for our family. Let's face it—we need everyone to make it all work. You get to define success for you, and I get to define success for me; it doesn't have to look the same.

What got us here won't get us to where we want to go. New thinking, diverse perspectives, inclusion, and tough conversations are all required to change the course we are on. This is the battle of my generation.

PART 3

THERE IS NO "I" IN T.E.A.M.

"Coming together is a beginning. Keeping together is progress. Working together is success."
—Henry Ford, *Inventor, Entrepreneur, Captain of Industry & Business Magnate*

T.E.A.M. **T**ogether **E**veryone **A**chieves **M**ore.

Cheesy and cliché, I know, and, at the same time, it's true. One person cannot achieve what a group of people is capable of achieving. One person can start a movement, inspire a generation, or make a discovery that changes the very future of our existence. For that idea, innovation, or invention to spread, to have an impact, and to inspire change, it requires a group of people. Tens of people, hundreds of people, or thousands of people, it doesn't matter; together, we achieve more than working alone.

Staff, employees, team members, the tribe, your peeps, whatever you call them, they are the people who look to you for vision, inspiration, and know-how. They are the reason you succeed or fail. And unless you are a solo-preneur, and I mean totally on your own 100% of the time, these next three chapters are all about building, maintaining, integrating, and engaging your team—in short, how to bring out the best in your people.

In the following chapters, I lay out the nuts and bolts of working with a team. You'll find suggested actions and reflections at the end of each concept, which I hope you find helpful for integrating the practice into your leadership. If it fits for you, wonderful. If it doesn't quite work, feel free to modify and adjust so that it does work for you.

CHAPTER 8 :
BUILDING AND MAINTAINING YOUR TEAM

"I can do things you cannot, you can do things I cannot;
together we can do great things."
—Mother Teresa, *Saint, Nun, Missionary*

Like it or not, leading a team comes with great responsibilities. Adding new team members, setting expectations, managing performance, and proactively restructuring the team to meet your goals are just a few of the tasks that will be required of you. As we've discussed throughout this book, the clarity of your vision, a deep understanding of your own skills and abilities, and effective communication are the keys to your success as you build, lead, and transform your team.

How Big? How Much?

What size is the right size for a team? When do you need assistants, other team leaders, or perhaps more structure? How many people can one effectively lead at any one time?

These are questions I'm sure we've all asked ourselves at various times in our careers and journeys. In my experience, one person can effectively lead anywhere from six to ten people directly. I have had as many as twenty-five team members and as few as one. In volunteer situations, I've lead teams as big as 50. The question isn't about how big of a team can I lead, but rather, how big of a team can I lead and still be effective?

I hate to tell you this, but the size of team you can lead effectively will depend on a lot of things: how much work there is to do; how much of the work you do yourself; the size of your company, organization, or business; the talent and skillset of your team members. All of these aspects influence how many people you can lead.

So here are some simple guidelines that have helped me over the years.

If I have a team of less than six, I have to ensure that I have some of the work do myself, or I will feel underutilized, bored, and complacent. I find that people in this space of quasi-leader are confused between do-er and lead-er, causing them to overcompensate and leaving the team feeling micro-managed. So, if you have a relatively small team, make sure you have tasks and deliverables of your own, to avoid the over-management of your team.

With a team of six to twelve people, I have found balance easily achieved. You have enough team members that the focus of your tasks as leader is providing vision and inspiration, and you have enough resources to execute work. Your time is spent strategizing, planning, and keeping the well-oiled machine of your team moving forward.

When I've led teams of more than 12, it's very easy to feel overworked, stretched too thin, and like there isn't enough of you to go around. It's hard to dive deep with all of your team members, so you find that the most vocal members get the most your time. You are barely able to scratch the surface of leading and can become tactical and impersonal. When in this situation, I often have feelings of being thrown off the deep end.

We all have a certain amount of bandwidth—energy and resources—to give in any given day, week, or month. If our team demands more than our bandwidth is able to provide, we will be less effective. It's as unique as we are, and it is a choice that everyone needs to make for themselves. Inside corporations, I believe that six to ten people per leader is an optimal use of resources, without over or under-utilizing any one resource.

Having the right-sized team allows for a leader to still have some time to produce their own work; however, the majority of their time will likely be spent on leading, guiding, developing, and engaging with their team. The reality is that no matter how much autonomy we provide to our team members, in order to get the work done, they still need some supportive structures to hold them, and they need to stay connected to the greater vision of the organization. This means that even if you are an entrepreneur hiring your first virtual assistant, you would be mistaken if you thought you could toss them the ball and walk away. In fact, in this situation, I'm betting that you are probably less likely to toss the ball to these new team members, as you normally wear this hat and have some pretty strong ideas on how things should be done. You're actually more likely to hover and micro-manage or to toss them the ball and take it right back at the first sign of trouble. Why? Because you haven't taken the time to detail what needs to be done, and to set up some lines of clear and open communication.

It is important to recognize your skills as a leader, but it is equally important to recognize your weaknesses. I don't point this out so that you spend vast amounts of time and effort and resources trying to shore up your weaknesses. I say this to highlight the fact that you should be looking to fill these gaps in your own leadership capabilities from inside your team. I've often been in a position on a team where I am not the direct leader, yet I am relied upon for my abilities to be empathic, to read the emotions in a room, and to tap into the underlying currents of what is truly happening within the team.

We can't do it all, and we simply cannot be everything everyone needs all of the time. It's an unattainable, unrealistic expectation and the longer we spend trying to perfect some area of weakness, the more time, energy, and resources are wasted. I invite you to spend some time to get to know what it is you do best, to assess what your team needs in this very moment, and to start seeking out the help, skills, and competencies you need. What can you delegate, outsource, or bring in to your team in order to excel?

Suggested Reflection:

If you find yourself wondering about the current structure of your team, take a few minutes and ask yourself the following questions. Write down the answers as they come to you in your journal or record them on a notes app in your phone.

1. How much time do I spend leading versus doing?

2. What are some tasks or deliverables I could delegate?

3. Do I have the skillsets in my current team to accept the work I wish to delegate?

4. What skillset(s) is my team missing?

5. Where can I add process or procedures to streamline?

6. Am I fully utilizing everyone on my existing team to the best of their current capabilities, skills, and strengths?

Come back to the answers before you make any hiring decisions, as they could influence your next hiring decision.

New Team Members

"We've got too much work. We need more people." I hear this all the time. When the work piles up and things become overwhelming, our first response is to throw more resources, often more people, at the issue and hope that things work out and become more manageable.

In reality, the exact opposite happens. We have a flood of new people join our team. Everyone is new, learning and trying to figure things out all at the same time. If you are the leader of this team, or the business owner, you will find that you can't offload what you thought you would. Mistakes are running rampant, and you are now actually more overwhelmed than before all this so-called help arrived. What went wrong?

In the moments of being overwhelmed, when things are seemingly out of control, we often revert to this mentality that if we just add more people, the problem will be solved. In fact, this is often the very best time to slow down, take a step back from the situation, and focus on what's really important. We become overwhelmed and out of control, from a lack of planning and direction. By spending time reviewing the current state of affairs, we can more accurately apply the correct solution.

So often when we interview people, we try to fit them into the role instead of offering the role we have to the right person. Are you able to see the difference here? It's subtle, yet so critical to hiring the right person and actually solving your problem of being overwhelmed and overworked. Be slow to hire. Once you have a role fleshed out and an idea of the skills, personality, and capabilities needed in your new team member, take your time during the hire process.

One effective strategy is to use multiple interviews by various people in the organization, to provide a more complete assessment of the candidates. Not everyone should go through all the interview rounds, but once you're down to a short list of potential people, get your current team involved. Who will the new team member work with the closest, and who will they need to collaborate with? Have these team members meet with the candidates, and then carefully consider their feedback and point of view. Conducting multiple interviews naturally slows down the process and allows for you to make the right hire, not just any hire.

Suggested Action:

Slow down to speed up. Set aside some time to read and reflect on the following questions, and see if you're able to start to fill out the skills and abilities the new member of your team would need to have.

1. What are the new hire's strengths?

2. What type of traits and values will the new hire need to have to complement and balance the team?

3. Who will this team member be accountable to?

4. What type of work environment do they need to be able to thrive?

Plan on at least three to four interviews for any new potential hire. Have multiple members of your organization or team meet with the new candidate and provide their assessments.

Some will only be able to comment on fit, while others will be able to comment on technical abilities. It's important that you get a good sense of how this person will complement the team you already have in place.

Veteran Team Members

The veterans, the old-timers, the lifers, the gray hairs, the rocks. It doesn't matter what you call them, they are the team members that have been there seemingly forever, the ones that know the ropes, who navigate the business with ease, and who seem to know everyone and everything. They can be your greatest ally or your most difficult obstacle as a leader. How you approach this resource on your team will determine whether they are friend or foe.

In my experience, veterans are an essential ally. The key in determining whether they will be an ally rather than an enemy lies in how you approach them. If you are a new leader to the team, or a new leader in a new company, the veterans on your team are a wealth of knowledge. Veterans often know more than the leader, and if you see this as a threat, you will either unconsciously, or perhaps very consciously, set up an adversarial relationship right from the start.

Not everyone aspires to lead. If you have veterans on your team, chances are they are in their long-standing roles for a reason. They aren't looking to climb a corporate ladder or go out on their own. They enjoy the comfort of being an expert in their chosen field, are grateful that someone else takes on all of the hassle of leadership, and, in most cases, are willing to help out as often as required in an unofficial leadership capacity.

Finding a way to access your experienced team members' knowledge of how things work, such as the political and social climate of the organization and the current challenges of the team, will be one of the keys to your success.

As painful as it is to lose brand-new hires, it is just as financially, and often more emotionally, difficult to lose veteran team members who have been with the company for several years. This may happen because new leadership hasn't assessed veterans' developmental level appropriately, but it more often happens because leadership has expectations that simply mismatch what the team member is willing to do.

Suggested Action:

Explore and implement ways to utilize the skills of your veteran team members that fill in the gaps of your abilities and leverage their strengths. Some suggestions are:

1. Pair veteran and new team members together in a mentoring program.

2. Have each team member present at a team meeting something that they're passionate about and that is relevant to the work the team is doing.

3. Have the veterans assist you in reviewing the business from time to time. They may see things that you have become too complacent to see, or may even spot things you would never notice.

4. Find out who on the team is aspiring to leadership and have them act as your second in command, with the support of your veteran team members. Not all veterans will want to be your second in command, but they can provide support while you are unable to fill your direct leadership role.

Integration

Integration is a pretty term that means "bringing together." Your ability to bring your team together, to integrate them, will be what defines your success or failure as their leader.

Can you recall the first day of a new job, the feeling of being the odd one out, wondering what in the world you've gotten yourself into, wandering around in search of the photocopier and washrooms, anxiously waiting for coffee and lunch breaks, and dashing out the door to head home at the end of the day? That first day is full of conflicting emotions, and, unfortunately, those feelings don't fade overnight. The first few weeks, sometimes months, are a time of transition, learning, and development, but they can also be full of excitement and enthusiasm. If for some reason you aren't finding anything to be genuinely excited about, you should probably keep your options open (but, that's a whole topic for a different book).

This integration of new team members is often referred to as onboarding. But, what does that even mean? I've experienced everything from having to read multiple four-inch binders filled with procedure manuals, to month-long, boot-camp style orientations. I've come to the conclusion that it is not the first few days that matter in the long run, but the experiences the new team member has during their first few months. And it's critical that you continue to meet with and include your veteran team members as the team grows and changes.

Statistically, companies are most likely to lose an employee or team member in the first two years of employment. Why? While there is a whole pile of research on this topic, it boils down to the fact that during the first two years in any new role—a new job, a first baby, a hobby—there is a natural and important phase during learning, where disengagement and the feeling of being overwhelmed takes over. When this phase of "What did I get myself into?" happens (and it will happen), the leader needs to recognize it and be able to support and encourage the team member through this time. The longer the team member stays in this house of pain, feeling frustrated, alone, and uncertain, the more checked-out and disengaged the team member becomes, and the risk of losing them increases dramatically. If the leader misses this key phase, they are likely to lose the employee. The team member has been mismanaged, either left to the wolves, micromanaged, or just plain misunderstood, due to lack of effective communication and connection.

There is a huge and often hidden cost to the turnover during this two-year period. An immense amount of money is spent on recruiting, hiring, and training a new employee, that isn't recovered until that employee has been with the organization longer than two years.

As leaders, we may miss a very subtle change in our new team members' development and learning, and in missing that change, we miss an opportunity to bond employees to the company and to our teams. The subtle change happens shortly after they're hired, when they begin to understand how much they don't know and how much they're going to have to learn. The fear and the questioning starts to settle in. This is the most time-consuming phase of development for your team members, but it's absolutely critical if we want to keep them engaged and performing well, that we spend the necessary time with them during this phase. This phase involves a lot of conversation, some detailed action planning, and a lot of confidence building. Basically, you become their biggest cheerleader. They will need some recognition and will need to know that they're doing a good job and making progress. In my experience, spending time with people during this phase is highly rewarding and builds bonds of trust and loyalty faster than any other activity I've ever tried as leader.

When you can develop your skills and abilities to a level where you can assess and diagnose your own development and needs, you've also reached a level where you deeply understand and appreciate what the people whom you lead are going through. You can more effectively adapt and apply the leadership style required to see this person through this stage of their own development, you will be quick to overcome challenging situations yourself, and you will acquire skills with great ease. Your ability to meet people where they are, show them new possibilities, and help them navigate the path of development, will strengthen significantly when you spend time really learning how to lead yourself.

Bottom line: leadership is about meeting people where they are at, understanding what they currently have access to, showing them new possibilities, and helping them develop the skills and abilities required to achieve these new possibilities.

Suggested Action:

Meet with team members one time per week. Make this a casual, informal meeting in a comfortable setting. I suggest asking the following questions and exploring the answers provided within your comfort level. Remember, sharing your own personal stories and anecdotes during these conversations may seem vulnerable (and it is!), but sharing yourself with others is what makes you human and relatable, and what bonds people together.

- What aspect of your current role is most rewarding to you?

- What aspect of your current role is most challenging for you?

- How can I support you in overcoming that challenge?

- What are you finding surprising about the role which you didn't expect?

- What do you view as your most valuable strength, and how are you able to utilize it currently in your role?

CHAPTER 9:
REDEFINING PERFORMANCE MANAGEMENT

*"Tell me and I'll forget. Show me and I may remember.
Involve me and I'll understand."*
—Chinese Proverb

Similar to how we, as companies, are shifting and changing our hiring processes, and how we are becoming more open and inclusive, our way of managing performance also needs to adjust and shift. If I have a company full of people who share similar demographics in terms of age and socioeconomic background, it's fairly safe to assume that they're probably going to have similar approaches to the tasks. Performance management, in this case, is fairly automatic and almost takes care of itself. Leaders could set the company goals, have a few performance targets, and turn people loose.

Fast forward to today's work environment, where we have five generations working together, a variety of socioeconomic backgrounds, a variety of ethnic backgrounds, and different genders all working together towards a common goal, and we still do performance management the way it was done 50 years ago. Say what?

Successful performance management looks like everybody on my team being utilized to their full capacity, engaged in their daily tasks and activities, and able, willing, and ready to perform at high levels, with the flexibility to meet the demands of their lives. Together, we reach all of our company-defined goals by being respectful, cooperative, and collaborative. It doesn't matter whether it's you and one virtual assistant, you and a team of 1,000 employees, you and your spouse with your 2.5 children, or you all by yourself training for a half-marathon; understanding what needs to be done and how it needs to be done, is the essence of performance management and critical to our success.

Say the words "performance management" in the corporate and entrepreneurial circles, and people cringe. I usually see two types of responses. The first is a shrug or deep sigh followed by, "Let's get on with it then. Things never change, and I don't get anything out of this process, but management says we need to do it, so let's get it over with." Or, I hear, "I don't do performance management. Period." Most people don't understand the purpose behind the performance discussion. They see it more as a pass/fail test than an invitation to a conversation, where deeper meaning and understanding are waiting to be discovered.

Performance management has gotten a bad rap over the years, which I believe is undeserving and unwarranted. Poor execution and a lack of understanding has led us right where we currently are, trying to help people grow and develop in their roles without the ability to build connections, develop understanding, or deliver our message with intention.

What Is Performance Management?

Have you ever trained for a sporting event—a running race, triathlon, bike race, walk to raise money to cure cancer, seven-day adventure hike where it's just you, your backpack, and the wilderness—anything? Maybe you have wanted to deliver an impactful speech to motivate your team, wow your senior leadership with a presentation on where your idea will take the business, or nail a sales pitch that will have crowds lining up to buy what you're selling? Have you ever wanted to write a book? (This last one is near and dear to my heart.)

What do all of these have in common? In order to achieve the goal or reach a desired outcome, we must manage our performance. When it comes to athletic achievement, we have to learn to read our bodies. We must find and maintain an optimal balance of nutrition, rest, and training. We must practice, accept coaching, implement feedback, and get up and try again. All professional sports teams have a team coach, and solo athletes hire performance coaches.

A professional setting is no different. People want and need to know how they are doing, what is going well, what needs improvement, and where to focus energy. We are hardwired to improve, to innovate, and to advance in our search for greatness. Yet, professionally, we struggle with this concept of performance management or coaching. I don't know where the ingrained behavior started, but I do know that I have felt this resistance to change, coaching, and improvement, especially when it comes to managing performance.

So, how do our team members get better, become more productive, and perform at higher levels? It would be foolish to believe this could be achieved with solely the support, coaching, and direction from the leader.

Instead, we must manage our performance by using information gathered from past behaviors and actions, to adjust our future behaviors and actions in service of achieving a different outcome. When we lead teams (professional, volunteer, families), we need to find and maintain the balance of preparation, practice, and strategy, adjusting as often as needed to keep moving forward in the pursuit of growth and innovation.

It baffles me when I run into leaders who think that their job is just to tell people what to do. In my experience, most people will often do exactly the opposite of what you want them to do if they don't understand why or how they need to do it. (If you have kids, you'll understand exactly what I mean by this.)

Suggested Action:

Conduct an informal audit of your performance management system for ease of use, participation, utilization, and effectiveness. Be prepared for the good, the bad, and the ugly in your feedback, and do something about it. If you're going to ask for feedback, be prepared to take action.

Setting Up the System

In order to lead someone (or many someones) to greatness, you will need a performance management system. It's not a nasty word, and it doesn't have to be scary. It just means you are setting yourself up for success by being organized. Your system should be simple, robust, and diligently executed.

My system is simple and robust, if executed with consistency. There are three parts:

1. Courageous Conversations

2. Thoughtful Feedback

3. Regular Cadence

That's it. No magic eight ball. No hocus pocus.

Courageous conversations are those conversations with our team members that stretch us as leaders. It may be telling someone that they didn't quite measure up, or it could be venturing into a subject you don't know a lot about but needs to be explored. These conversations can be difficult and uncomfortable; they are deeply vulnerable, and they most definitely force us outside our comfort zones. Being courageous means praising someone who we feel threatened by instead of belittling and judging them like we so often want to do. It means telling someone the same thing in eight different ways, ten different times, hoping this time they actually hear your message. Courageous conversations are those conversations we may dread having and so often put off. Sometimes, they are also those conversations we deem unnecessary, because the other person must know how wonderful they are doing.

Your team, your spouse, and your kids don't know what you're thinking. You have to tell them the good, the bad, and the ugly. You have to engage in a conversation, outlining the goal and the expectations and monitor how they're doing. Engaging in conversation consists of two parts: setting the expectation or goal, and ongoing monitoring with check-ins and evaluations of the performance related to that goal. We build up these conversations in our minds so much, that we get scared and retreat. I've often told myself, "It's not really as bad as you're making it out to be," or "You don't need to say anything, because they already know how great they're doing," or "Of course, they know what we're working towards, so we don't need to write it down." If you find yourself thinking these same thoughts, stop! You cannot be an effective leader if you aren't willing to step up, take action despite your fears, celebrate the high points, encourage throughout the low points, and speak the truth.

Being courageous is also about feedback. It's one thing to book the conversation, and it's an entirely different thing to exchange feedback that is meaningful and timely. Insightful and thoughtful feedback takes work. Engaging in a conversation requires you to have questions prepared that are thought-provoking, and that stretch people to see something that was previously out of their line of sight. To be able to offer feedback, you have to observe someone's work through the lens of what you can offer, to raise the impact of their action or words. This is a skill of a true leader.

I recommend approaching giving feedback to someone in consideration of a) what will serve them best or b) how your feedback can be of service in what they are trying to achieve. If you can hold this intention at the core of your feedback, it will usually hit the mark and be more readily received. When we approach feedback from the perspective of "do it my way" or "be more like me," it doesn't honor the individuality, personality, or strengths of the other person. Leadership is not about you. It's about the people who are following you and looking to you for direction, inspiration, and vision. If you don't work on being that person for them, why would they work on becoming the person you need them to be?

Imagine you're at your birthday party, and it's time to open gifts. Someone has taken the time to carefully (or maybe not so carefully) select and wrap a gift for you. When you open it, do you throw up the shields of defense, or do you accept the gift? Regardless of whether you'll actually use the gift or not, I'm willing to bet that most of us graciously accept the gift, even if we're trying to figure out the first opportunity we'll have to re-gift or donate the item to a worthier cause.

Feedback is a gift. Your job is to offer the feedback, and the team member's job is to accept it, even if it might not fit. It might not match their interior design, and it might seem totally useless at the time, like the singing trout wall ornament your uncle gave you for your birthday, but it's still a gift. Do not disrespect each other by either withholding the feedback or throwing it away once it's given.

Receiving feedback is a tricky business. There are two fundamental types of feedback: solicited and unsolicited. Most of us will raise the shields of defense and immediately prepare for battle when someone offers us unsolicited feedback. But it, too, is a gift. Helping your team members understand and embrace the gift in the feedback, will help them accept and act upon the suggestions you are offering.

Solicited feedback is often easier to accept; after all, we've asked for it. For me, I often know the gist of the feedback I'm going to get in situations where I asked for it. Rarely do I get out of left field surprises. With solicited feedback, the defenses are lower, although not completely gone, and the acceptance of feedback is easier, but not immediate. One will likely still need assistance finding the gift in the advice offered. Know that, as the recipient of the feedback, you get to choose what you do with it.

Years ago, Matthew and I received a wedding gift that was a metal, nine-by-thirteen inch, stainless steel baking pan with a rack—totally unimpressive and generic. I remember thinking as I opened it that I had no idea how or when I would use it, and I could easily leave it at my mom's house and never have to see it again. Matthew said we were taking it home. Someone had gone out, picked out the gift, and wrapped it up, and that act deserved our respect. Fast forward and here we are, years later, and that pan has been a pivotal part of my family. Many meals have been cooked in that pan, everything from lasagna and to rice crispy squares, and it's still going strong. I've even taught my kids to cook with that pan. I could have easily dismissed this seemingly unimpressive gift, but thanks to my husband's wisdom, it has become an integral part of my family's kitchen.

I use this story to illustrate that so often, we act before we accept. We dismiss, we defend, and we diminish. I'm urging you to help your team members learn how to accept the feedback first. Teach them that accepting is not agreeing; rather, it is saying thank you and being receptive. Allow them time to reflect on the feedback and the intention, and the underlying motivations with which it was given.

Feedback, like a gift, is always given from the giver's perspective. My baking pan was given to me by a dear friend who had raised a family and probably knew exactly how important that piece of metal would become to my family. Because I did not yet share her perspective, I didn't see it. Be careful what you throw out, what you put in storage, and what you act upon. You never know when someone will give you a piece of feedback that will change the very course of your actions and quite possibly your life.

Here are some questions you can offer your team members to use when reflecting upon feedback:

- What is the intent of this feedback?

- What can I learn from this information?

- How will this help me lead myself and others?

If they find nothing in the feedback of substance, ask them to let it go. Our perspectives, advice, and insights are just ours. Likely, the feedback you offer team members isn't going to land 100% of the time. Teach them through sharing your own experiences to take the juicy, insightful tidbits, run with them, and let go of the rest.

I encourage you to be open to receiving feedback about your actions and behaviors from your team members. This performance management conversation is a great place to ask for a few specific examples of what's going well for your team member, and what could use improvement. You won't always like the feedback, but, if you're aiming to be a highly effective leader and one who leads with empathy, you will realize what a gift these insights are and treasure them like the precious commodity they are. Feedback is a two-way street. You have to be able to give it and take it.

Performance management, our courageous conversations and feedback gifts, is not a one-time event, nor is it one-size-fits-all. This brings us to the third part of the system: cadence.

Cadence is the beat, rate, or measure of any rhythmic movement. One team member might require one meeting per year, and it takes you 45 minutes. Another might require monthly meetings that are three hours long each. We are all unique, and we all have different requirements to reach our goals and be our best. It's your job as the leader to figure out the required cadence of courageous conversations and thoughtful feedback, and then execute them. Failure to execute both will result in less than desired performance, every time. I guarantee it.

As a general rule, if you are uncertain where to begin, a quarterly conversation is a good place to start, and you should plan for two to four hours per person. The two to four hours will not all be spent face-to-face with your team member. Some of that time will allow for you to review the past performance, to reflect on behaviors and actions, and to determine where you want to take the conversation. The conversation itself will likely run one to two hours, depending on what's coming up and topics which need to be discussed. At the end, I recommend taking 30-45 minutes to reflect on the conversation, doing an assessment of your performance (yes, this is your own feedback to yourself), and noting what you will observe and work toward with this team member in the coming months.

As this is a system and should be set up as process in your business, team, or company, I recommend you have a way to record the conversation, the feedback, and the agreement to the timing of each conversation. This can be as simple as writing things out on a sheet of paper or a spreadsheet, or as involved as implementing a full software solution. The solution will depend on what you have available to you. If you work inside an established organization, this process will likely be administered by your Human Resources group. If you are a business owner, you will have to decide when it's time to move from "everyone knows what needs to be done" to a more formal system. Again, there is no one-size-fits-all. If what you are currently doing works for you, keep doing it. If it doesn't work any longer, implement some of the suggestions here, and see where it takes you.

I know this sounds like a lot, and it can be overwhelming at first, but here's a simplified version. Commit to the conversation. Offer the feedback and observations. Stay open to improvement. Record. Repeat regularly.

Over time, you will develop and strengthen your skills, and your team members will also become more skilled, creating the momentum your team requires to become truly high performing.

Suggested Action:

Build or refine your performance management system.

1. Set up a place to write down and track goals, tasks, or actions. It may be an online system, a spreadsheet, or sticky notes on your bathroom mirror. It doesn't matter where or how you do this, it just matters that you do it.

2. Plan and execute your courageous conversation. Talk about your performance with another human being. If you are a leader, drive this conversation. If you are running a business alone, hire a coach, get a mentor, or book time with another business owner and swap services.

3. Give and accept the feedback. Confirm what actions you are leaving the conversation with. Keep doing what's working and adjust what isn't working.

4. Get your next conversation in the calendar to build the cadence.

Managing Your Own Performance

It's so easy to look out the window, and judge and blame others for our situation, our actions, and even our words. This may sound a bit far-fetched, and yet, I find myself and others blaming those around us for the words that come out of our own mouths. My children often push me past the point of my own limits, and I have found myself on more than one occasion lashing out in anger or deep frustration, blaming them for my fierce words. It takes a tremendous amount of energy and effort to focus on our own conscious thoughts, to look in the mirror at ourselves, and truly understand that we hold the power in our situation.

How does the old saying go, hindsight is always 20/20? In those situations at home or at work where I find myself lashing out, I have come to understand that when I'm so deeply frustrated or angry at a particular situation, behavior, or action of someone else's, it is often due of my own fatigue, hunger, or lack of presence. In these times, I have no room to assess and choose my reaction, so I act outwardly, impulsively, and recklessly.

Through practicing the skills of being present and looking at what I bring to the situation, I have noticed that if I am rested, nourished, and connected, I can bring an abundance of patience and understanding to a situation. It doesn't mean that I let my kids or team members off the hook; rather, I can lead, guide, teach, and set and boundaries with a quiet confidence that sometimes scares people. People don't react to my yelling and screaming the same way as when I'm firm, calm, and speaking in an even voice. People sense and know the difference when I approach a conversation, either blaming them in error or taking responsibility for my part, and your team will too.

The more you learn about yourself, the more you learn about others, and it cannot help but positively influence the situations you find yourself in. Once we begin to become aware and curious about our own actions, words, and behaviors, we want to move either towards something or away from something. This takes effort. When to exert the effort, what style of effort, and the intensity of your effort is often hard to determine on your own. This is where assessments, training, mentoring, and coaching are all excellent tools in your leadership toolbox to call upon. For each of us, it takes a different balance of these tools. Try on a few and see what works. Stay open and curious. Establishing your baseline and having some written goals for how you want to improve, will help you check in and monitor your progress. In order to be effective in the shortest amount of time possible, you need to know how, where, and when to act, and you'll likely need outside support to answer these questions.

Finally, reflection, awareness, and focusing your efforts takes practice. You should not expect to master a skill or technique the first time. I'm guilty of having this expectation of myself to master something the first time, and sometimes of others, but I also know it is unrealistic and unattainable. Carrying this expectation has left me disappointed on more than one occasion. Do you know what is attainable and realistic? Taking 10,000 hours of practice to build mastery. For example, I will have over 10,000 hours invested in this book by the time I finish it, between the experience, research, and writing. It won't be perfect (I'm working on letting go of that expectation, so that a book actually gets written) and yet, I'll be a better writer and leader than before. After 10,000 hours of dedicated practice, disciplined effort, and consistent implementation of empathic leadership, you will be better too.

Suggested Action:

Ask your team for feedback. The common term is a 360° review, which is a fancy name for a system to gather anonymous feedback on your performance as a leader. It should come from both those you lead and those who lead you. There are vast resources—websites, toolkits, apps, software systems—to do this work, or it could be as simple as an online survey. Don't make it complicated, but do make it a priority.

Suggested Reflection:

Keep a journal: electronical, pen and paper, or voice memos. Have some record for yourself of what you were going through, what's working, and what's not. Try and make an entry at least once per week. Re-read entries as often as you like, but at least one or two times per year.

Managing Your Team's Performance

Leading a team.

Three small words, quite simply stated. And yet, in practice, it is one of the most difficult things to do. Learning how to listen to what's really being said and not just hearing the words which are spoken. Learning how to open up ourselves to vulnerability and be firm in our vision at the same time.

Cultivating a curiosity to learn about your team members as people, outside their resume and education. These are the skills that build connections, inspire movements, and move teams from average to high performance.

Early in my career, I led a team of twelve engineers and technical sales representatives for about three years. It was the first time I had worked with a truly diverse team across domains of gender, marital status, ethnic culture, professional experience, religion, and personality. While twelve people may seem like a small team to some, to me, it was a rich tapestry in which I could learn about myself and others.

One time I was conducting phone interviews with potential candidates in the Middle East. We were a global company, and people often moved between countries to advance their careers within the organization. Having a name like Erin, people often assume I'm a male, and one candidate was very surprised to hear my female voice on the phone. He quickly stated that he could not work for a female leader and that if I were the only option, he would not come to Canada. It was an amicable phone call, albeit short. I found myself grateful for his honesty.

That was one of the defining moments, where I became fully aware that my gender played a role in my leadership journey. I remember sitting there questioning it and then quickly dismissing the notion that just because I was a girl, I couldn't lead. This was not my issue.

As a Canadian, born and raised, there is common understanding between us in the way in which we speak to each other, which tends to be indirect and uses suggestions to try to get people to see our point of view and influence behavior. When I lead teams of second or third generation Canadians, this approach usually works well because of the common communication style we share. However, when I was coaching and trying to lead first-generation Canadians who had just emigrated from other countries, this approach was highly ineffective. first-generation Canadians are used to much more directive and commanding types of leadership, which I find extremely uncomfortable, overbearing, and aggressive, because of my experience as a child with my own command and control leadership style. I still had some work to do on when and where I employed different styles to maximize my effectiveness.

As I moved into the work place and started to lead my own teams and to be led by other people, I quickly realized that the dictator was not who I identified with, and was not the person that I wanted to be. I didn't enjoy being led by command and control leaders, and I didn't think that it was the best way to get things done. So, I actually became the exact opposite. I became more a delicate, hands-off, silent leader, but this came with its own challenges. When I delegated or adopted a hands-off approach, team members didn't always know what was expected of them or how to do it. It took me a while to figure out, embrace, and implement the middle ground, which I quickly glossed over in my learning.

During those early years of my career, as I began to discover and understand how I was showing up when it came to leading others, I became very self-conscious about being aggressive, dominant, and overbearing. These weren't positive words in my vocabulary, and I certainly didn't want them to be associated with me any longer, especially as I started to become more aware of the ineffectiveness of this leadership style in most situations, outside of emergencies and life-or-death situations.

I had spent years working hard to build new leadership skills, and to find new ways to achieve similar results that I had achieved with command and control. During this phase of my own development, the pendulum swung a bit too far in the other direction. I had buried my dominance traits and had worked hard to develop a more influencing style of leadership, which meant that I couldn't call on the skills I once had. I would need to tap into a part of me that I had long forgotten about, in order to lead strong, dominant people from different cultures. Some of my team members needed me to be direct, so that they could hear what I was saying, and I needed to be assertive with them, perhaps even more forceful than I was comfortable with. I needed a clear and concise message without added niceties or minced words.

Once I tapped into my command and control style from my early years and applied it with a bit more finesse, I was able to communicate with my team members in a way they could hear what I had to say. It was magic. Amazing things started happening in our team. Everyone began to hear what I was saying and see what I was seeing. They began to implement the strategies and direction I was giving them. Overall, as our trust in each other increased, so did our results.

I had to be intentional with what type of leadership skills I applied and when. If I was talking to people on my team who were second or third generation Canadians and who communicated like me, all it would take was a mere suggestion or a hint at different actions, and the team member could hear and implement what I was asking. I was beginning to see that delivering the same messages to diverse people in different ways, so that they could hear me, was the key to being effective. I knew what I wanted as the outcome, and if the person couldn't receive the message because of the way I was delivering it, then I had the ability to change the delivery.

My ability to manage someone's performance was put to the test early in my career, when I had to performance manage my former mentor (you may remember this story from Chapter 3). At first, the conversations with the individual were light, focused, and professional. As time went on, I began to see that my position as leader of our team was not truly respected. Our meetings were being canceled at the last minute or blown off altogether, and actions and behaviors we had agreed on during our face-to-face meetings were not changing outside our conversations. In a word, he was showing me that he was either unwilling to be coached or just simply was not coachable. I ended up having to terminate my former mentor, having been his leader for a year.

This truly was one of the hardest things I've ever had to do in my career, and it was one of the things that taught me the most about myself, my abilities, my strengths, and my weaknesses. I had a very emotional response through this whole thing (I am an empathic leader after all), but what I learned through it was how to use the framework I have laid out for you in this book: to have the conversations that were required to address the business needs, without making it a personal attack. You often hear business is business, personal is personal, people are people. But people contain multitudes related to both work and personal life. We are whole human beings, not to be separated out, sliced and diced into whatever situation we happen to be working in, and when we happen to be working in it.

As the leader of my team, it is up to me to have the vision of where we are headed and to have an understanding of how we are going to get there. The same is true for you. It is our job to know our team members, to understand them as whole people, and then to adjust our approach in a way that serves them best. If we are going to achieve great things, each person on every team needs to be heard, supported, inspired, and motivated.

Usually, leaders (this includes me) use the team meeting forum to go over what's required from the team, and to pass along relevant information. This works for getting the word out, but if you have team members who are new to your team or who you know need the personal one-on-one follow up, make it a priority to touch base with them as soon as you can after the meeting. This will ensure that they have a chance to ask any questions they may have, and you can confirm that they received the message as you intended to deliver it. I used to rely solely on the team meeting environment to communicate with my teams, and, over time, I learned to communicate in multiple forums and different ways so that could I get my message out to each person.

Whatever it is you use to measure and monitor success in your business—sales number, new subscribers, units sold, production numbers, people recruited—it only gives you half the story of what's really going on in the business. When things are going well, it's easy to not look any further than these business metrics. It's comfortable to sit back and see a well-oiled machine running at peak performance. Don't fall into this trap. You are able to hit the numbers for a reason, and that reason is your team. When the numbers aren't there and things aren't so noteworthy, it's for the same reason: your team.

Stay connected to your people, celebrate the wins, share in the disappointments, and keep them connected to their work. Your most critical tasks is to help them understand why what they do is important, and how it impacts the metric you use to measure success. After all, there is no "I" in team.

Suggested Action:

Stay connected. Weekly informal coffee meetings, a monthly breakfast gathering where you rotate through the team members to teach on a topic that they are passionate about and that's relevant to the team, and regularly scheduled formal performance management check-ins, are all effective ways of staying in touch and connected to what is happening with your team.

Be authentic. As much as you can, share what's going on with you, what's going well in the business and in your life, and where are your challenges. You never know who on your team may have the key to unlocking a situation until you share and ask.

CHAPTER 10: INCREASING ENGAGEMENT

"Happy employees ensure happy customers. And happy customers ensure happy shareholders—in that order."
—Simon Sinek, *Author, Speaker, Marketing Consultant*

Whether you are given a team, inherit a team, or build a team from scratch, there are a number of moving parts you'll need to pay attention to as their leader. Engagement is one of the most important, if not the most important. And it's a pretty hot topic in the leadership circles right now, as it should be, since employee engagement is directly linked to revenue growth.

Employee engagement is defined as a workplace approach resulting in the ideal conditions for all members to give their best each day, be committed to the team's goals and values, stay motivated to contribute to overall success, and have an enhanced sense of their own well-being.

While a far greater conversation on this topic is taking place outside this book, there are two key points I would like to make. First, look at where engagement starts, and, second, put the first point into action. Companies conduct surveys every year and, in most cases, they have little to no effect on actual employee engagement. Employee engagement starts with the relationship between two people, so if you want to increase employee engagement, start with your own team. Start by connecting, listening, and doing what needs to be done.

Where Engagement Starts

Engagement starts with trust.

It's our job as leaders to look for signs of disengagement. Decreased communication, increased frustration, employee absenteeism, and—my all-time favorite—total radio silence, are all signs we need to pay attention to. The single most critical sign that I have a team member who is losing engagement, is that they stop asking questions. I know that when they have stopped asking questions, they now understand how much they don't know. They're scared to let anyone else see how vulnerable they are, and their confidence has totally tanked. In short, they don't trust me as their leader to help them, they don't trust themselves to be able to do the work, and they don't trust that the organization will have their back.

Sometimes, we get uncomfortable when we encounter team members in this stage of development, because we confuse their competence with their ability to learn. If we hire people who are motivated and able to learn, they will be able to be successful in the role. Where we often fall short as leaders, is that we expect them to come to the table with the skills already in hand.

Having a strong foundation of knowledge is essential, but we all have to learn the new skills that are required to be successful in a new role, team, and company. It's like expecting that your 12-year-old son will somehow know how to do his laundry just because he wears clothes. Chances are, he might know where the washer and dryer are, but he will have no clue how to turn them on, or that they require things like soap and fabric softener. As for sorting, well, let's just say there will be a lot of interestingly colored laundry if he is left figure it out on his own. Wearing clean clothes for 12 years doesn't mean he knows how they get cleaned, but, once he is developmentally ready, he's in a position to learn how to do the laundry with the help of leadership, coaching, and feedback. He'll start with a level of enthusiasm that might just surprise you, when you show him how to load and fill the machines the first time, and eventually he'll graduate to doing it by himself. Somewhere in the next few weeks or months, he'll become disengaged after the luster of turning on the washer wears off. He may stop doing the laundry all together and go back to wearing wrinkled clothes from his floor. He will go silent.

Employee disengagement is a natural element when you lead a team; once we learn to embrace it and understand how to leverage it, by helping our team members learn and move through the discomfort, it becomes the single most effective tool that bonds people to their organizations and leaders. Having clearly-defined expectations, autonomy to do work aligned with preferences, and some cheering-on along the way, all play a part in keeping people engaged in organizations. Even those of us in the leader's seat will go through a period of disengagement from time to time. It's up to us, in those moments, to diagnose what is needed, seek guidance, and get busy learning a new skill. We are, after all, whole people.

True leaders meet people where they need to be met and help them walk the path ahead. We must adapt our leadership style to the needs of our team if we're going to be truly effective and engaging. Leadership also requires an ability on our part to be vulnerable and to share our own experiences, so that our team members can see a way through their current situation.

In order to be effective at re-engaging team members, it's important to customize your approach based on their personality, their communication style, and the needs of the situation. This is what I refer to as the art and science of leadership. The science of leadership encompasses the many models, frameworks, structures, and processes that should, in theory, be all we need to keep our teams engaged and feeling supported. However, we are human. Everyone is going to have their own unique experiences, perspectives, thoughts, and feelings. The art of leadership exists in the application our knowledge, skills, and experiences, and the recognition that each of us is a unique individual and must be treated as such. Blending both the art and the science creates magic, and teams move from mediocrity to high performing at the speed of light, due to the high degree of trust that exists. Your team needs to trust you, and you need to trust them. Trust is built one act at a time by doing what you say and saying what you mean. By seeing people for who they really are, valuing their perspectives and contributions, and by hearing their unique voice, you honor their individuality. These actions build trust.

In the larger conversation about leadership, too often, we talk about "our" way of leading. It's important to know how we show up and who we are (which is why I recommend *Strengths Finder 2.0*), but we also need to consider that we all have one way of leadership that we commonly practice under normal circumstances, and another way of leadership that we practice when we're under stress. What I don't hear enough about in the conversation is this notion of being able to adapt to the situation or circumstance, and if we're intent on being consistently good leaders, we'll have to learn the skills needed to adapt our style of leadership to stressful situations.

If I look back to when I was the kid and how I showed up in my family and tried to lead my siblings, I truly was a dictator. It was my way or the highway! I thought that everything needed to be done in a certain, precise way and, of course, my way was the best. Things had to be done in my time, to my schedule, to my liking. As important as it is to know your own strengths and weaknesses, leadership isn't about what you, as a leader, need. Leadership is about what your team members need to get things done; it's about gaining awareness and understanding of your own skills and experiences, and doing your absolute best to meet people where they are. In between the extremes of the dictator and the hands-off delegator, two competencies are critical to our toolboxes (and you'll notice that both are predicated on the skills of listening and connecting talked about earlier in the book).

The first competency is being able to support people. Support involves providing detailed instructions on what needs to be done, and also helping bolster their motivation and commitment to the situation, task, or team. What would this look like? It looks like a conversation between you and your team member, arriving at a prescriptive set of tasks and then checking in with your team member along the way, providing support and camaraderie. Basically, it's cheering them on until they've achieved what needs to be done, or until they've learned new skills. This is a very time-consuming part of leadership. It's often required with newer employees or people who are newer to tasks, after they've had some time to get to know the inner workings of the team and their required duties. Remember the example of the business report? This type of leadership would have gone a long way in making sure that everyone was on the same page, and producing positive outcomes for both parties involved.

The second type of leadership competency is coaching. In the truest sense of the word, coaching embodies being able to highlight what other people can't see and showing them a different way to achieve what deeply matters to them. Coaching means having conversations around mindset and increasing motivation, by showing the team member that they actually have the competencies to do this work. It's more about showing them that they can trust themselves and less about prescribing a set of actions or tasks that need to be carried out. Your team member will generally know what needs to be done in most situations; they just might lack the confidence to go out and do it.

My favorite model for leadership that I've run across in the last 10 years is the Situational Leadership II model by Ken Blanchard. This model outlines four stages of development that every person will go through in any given situation. Team members will move through the development stages more quickly or effectively with greater outcomes, if the leader is able to match the leadership style with the development level.

Situational Leadership II provides a leadership language and framework that is based on outcomes and focused on behaviors. This simple yet effective framework has four development levels and four complementary leadership styles, illustrated in a matrix layout; essentially, the y-axis represents supportive behaviors and the x-axis represents directive behaviors, both ranging from low to high. The matrix results in four types of leadership styles to match learners' developmental levels, in order from least-developed to most-developed: directing (high directive, low supportive), coaching (high directive, high support), supporting (low directive, high supportive), and delegating (low directive, low supportive). The leadership style moves along a curve, beginning with high directive behavior, gradually increasing supportive behavior, and eventually decreasing both directive and supportive behaviors as the learner fully develops. You can find more information and a diagram of the model at www.kenblanchard.com/Products-Services/Situational-Leadership-II.

The beauty of this model lies in its utter simplicity. Consider the example from Chapter 5 where I asked my new team member to prepare the business report with a less-than-desirable outcome. My new team member was highly committed to the tasks but lacked competence, which reflects the first level of development known as an "enthusiastic learner" (high commitment, low competence). To be an effective leader for a team member in the first level of development, I needed to be directive in my leadership style. If I would have outlined the task and deliverable, specifically and in detail, we would have both had a much more enjoyable experience. Why? In short, I would have been adapting my leadership style to match my team member's development, meeting my team member where they were in their development as a learner.

Keep in mind that this framework is called situational for a reason. The assessment of development should be applied to each situation or task that the team member faces. This sounds overwhelming at first; however, in most positions on a team, there are a handful of key tasks or situations that a person will be required to carry out to be successful in their role. My advice is to focus on these key situations, assess frequently (once per quarter), and adjust leadership styles to match development as required.

What's at stake if the leader isn't properly assessing a team member's developmental level? You might hear things like, "Oh Joe, he's been here for 30 years, he knows everything about this," or, "Sarah? Ya, she's brand-new. We really need to go and give her the details of what needs to be done around here." Turns out, Joe might've been working for the company for 20 years but has no idea how Windows 10 works, and is deeply struggling in trying to figure out his place in this organization as new technology is introduced, trapped in the house of pain. Joe really needs some support and guidance to get him through these next phases in his own development. Sarah, on the other hand, might be brand-new to the team but has been doing the assigned task for 10 years in other industries, and knows the ins and outs like the back of her own hand. She's feeling micromanaged and is wondering why people don't trust her skills and ability.

Hopefully, you can start to see from these brief examples how applying broad generalizations to people's abilities and needs is dangerous and doesn't help the team, the leader, or the organization move forward and can, in fact, end up setting you back, which means starting over and forever trying to get off the ground.

Suggested Action:

Read *The One Minute Manger* by Ken Blanchard and start to be curious about how you could adapt your style to meet the needs of your team.

Actions Speak Louder than Words

Talk the talk. Walk the walk. Find and embrace the power in walking the talk.

Nothing is more damaging to trust and credibility than saying one thing and doing the exact opposite. When companies say they care about people and then cut back social programs, it kills engagement, ruins trust, and cripples teams. As team members, rationalizing the story can be difficult when we aren't privy to the why behind a decision. We don't understand the story, and, in the absence of understanding, we make up our version of the truth to help us justify what's happening in our world.

I have always been pleasantly surprised by people's positive reactions when I have to explain a decision or direction that could be difficult to accept, if I start by helping them understand the drivers behind the decision. I approach situations this way, because it's easier for me to understand something if I have some sense of why it's happening. You may come across people who don't need to understand why and will take direction without question; in my experience, though, this is rare (with the exception of life or death situations). I try to put myself in their place and honor their unique experience, perspective, and background, to help me communicate in a way that will help my message be heard.

To build and maintain engagement, we must be willing to follow through on what we say we will do. If a change is required in the team and we've publically committed to making the change, do it. Whatever it takes, make sure you follow through. If you want to see a change in your team or your company, you have to be willing to make that change yourself. So, if you wish your team was more engaged, perhaps you should consider becoming more engaged with them. In large part, the urgency I felt to walk the talk is why this book exists.

For over a decade, I have felt that leadership in the industries I've travelled in could be more effective. A few years ago, I realized I had skills and a story that could be used to further this effort, but crippling fears and self judgements prevented me from doing anything about it. It wasn't until I was sitting in a conference in 2012 that an unsolicited thought popped into my head: "You should be on that stage. You should be sharing your story and making an impact." At the time, I quickly dismissed this thought and talked myself out of this crazy, ridiculous idea. And for four years, every time I had this idea or thought about using my own experiences and story to help spread the message, I would squash it down or shoo it away, until I couldn't any longer.

I realized that if I wanted to see change, I had to join the conversation. I had to overcome my fears that someone, or many someones, may disagree with me. I had to get serious about the message: my beliefs, my thoughts, and my actions. I had to do the uncomfortable work of getting to know myself at a deeper level, connecting the experiences with the learnings and the skills with the actions. In short, I couldn't just talk about a different way to lead; I had to step into it and show people, and I had to put into practice exactly what I believed in. In the time I've been working on this book, I have witnessed a profound impact on my family, my teams, and my own fulfillment.

I know now that there is no formula to life, and no one else can give you the roadmap to your journey. All you can do is take the next step you know to be right and see where you end up. It's critical to stay tuned into your own emotions and your own physical manifestations. If you are able to quiet your mind and listen to your body, you can tap into your unique and authentic GPS system, which will take you places you never dreamed possible.

Mahatma Gandhi said, "Be the change that you wish to see in the world." The meanings behind these words finally sunk in one day in 2016 while I sat in a coffee shop, working on my business plan. That persistent voice inside, urging me to share my story, started talking once again, but, this time, the voice said to write a book. Say what?! I sat there thinking, "You can't be serious." I had worked my whole life up to this point to avoid writing anything. My entire career was based on a decision founded in the belief that I was not good at writing. I went to engineering school to avoid using my high school English marks, which were average at best. Yet, on this particular day, I did something different. I was ready to make a change, so I found a writing coach, booked a call, and committed to getting this book written. While I don't know where things will go from here, I can confidently claim my spot on the team that is bringing more awareness, more connection, and more feeling—in short, more empathy—to leadership. I have engaged. I am part of the change I wish to see in this world.

PART 4

PRACTICE MAKES YOU ~~PERFECT~~ BETTER

*"Success has to do with deliberate practice.
Practice must be focused, determined, and in an environment
where there's feedback."*
- Malcolm Gladwell, *Journalist, Author, Speaker*

The road to embracing empathy is long and winding. At times, you may feel like you are moving backward and like you should give up. I know I've felt that way. The following illustration has been my go-to image over the years when I try anything new, because it represents how the path in our minds rarely matches the path in reality.

PATH TO SUCCESS

IN MY MIND

REALITY

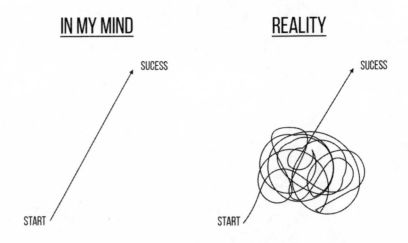

What's most surprising is that the pile of spaghetti standing between start and success is actually where the magic happens. It's chaotic and uncomfortable, but it's where we learn the power of seeing people as they are and of asking a question with the intention of listening deeply to the response. I didn't expect that wading through the mess, I would receive the rich rewards that practicing empathy would bring to my life.

The generic list of benefits of practicing empathy is vast (just google it); however, I wanted to make this a bit more personal by sharing with you a few of the many benefits that I have gained by uncovering and embracing my superpower: empathy.

- I have a richly rewarding and powerful partnership with my husband that allows us to lean on each other, recognizing and celebrating our different perspectives and experiences, which would have likely driven us crazy without an effective tool to communicate, listen, and connect.

- I am able to connect deeply with my children and help them see their differences as strengths.

- I am a happier and more fulfilled wife, mother, sister, daughter, and friend.

- I am more effective in my leadership

- I have successfully lead diverse teams, at least in part by creating an environment of inclusivity.

- I am a valuable resource to other leaders in my organizations who don't possess the skills I do in emotional intelligence.

- I have the ability to treat others as they wish to be treated, without judgement or hesitation.

- I am curious about individuals as a whole person and actively seek to understand them just as they are.

- I am less attached to others' emotions, which in turn allows me to be able to hold space for both myself and others and keep our emotions separate.

- I am able to honor my own callings and desires.

- I am stepping up and saying "yes!" to sharing my story and my experiences, with the intention of showing others how to embrace their own truths.

- I am writing this book, despite the self-doubt and fears.

CHAPTER 11 : EMPATHY FOR OTHERS

"Instead of putting others in their place,
put yourself in their place."
—Amish Proverb

The core principles of this book are centered around empathic leadership. Empathy is not a style of leadership; rather, empathy is woven into all styles of leadership.

If we can't meet someone where they are and truly stand in their shoes, in order to understand what it is like to experience their day from their point of view, we will not be as effective or as fulfilled in our role as leaders. Difficult discussions would be even more difficult, performance management would become a nightmare, turnover and attrition would become your life, and you would spend most of your time hiring and firing instead of inspiring.

Picture an iceberg. We only see about 20% of an iceberg floating above the surface of the water. The performance of your team is the tip of the iceberg; performance is what we can see and what we can measure. The other 80% that exists below the surface, is the rest of the whole human beings, who show up every day and perform tasks and duties required to make your team successful. Empathy allows you to see people below the surface. It equips you to treat this individual as a unique, whole person and provide the guidance, coaching, and support they need (even if it's a kick out of the nest). Empathy allows you to meet people where they need to be met and to keep them inspired to continue on the journey with you.

Let's face it, not everybody is meant to be on our journey with us; they may have their own path to follow. I consider it a success when I can grow and develop someone who goes on to surpasses my achievements and accomplishments. Nothing brings me greater joy or satisfaction than watching a team member spread their wings and fly away, starting their own journey as a leader of a new team, an owner of a small business, or an entrepreneur starting a new venture.

I use assessments as one of the tools in my leadership toolbox, not to paint people into a box or to assign a label, but to provide a perspective of this unique individual, which I might not otherwise see. I use this information when entering into conversations with my team members, so we can communicate successfully. Many times we go into conversations, especially around performance management, saying something to the effect of, "I've noticed Y and it doesn't look like X", where "Y" is the other person's way and "X" is my way. It's the old trap of my-way-or-the-highway mentality.

It's better to simply ask the person how they think they're doing, what's going well, and what's most challenging for them. Most people who I've worked with have a pretty good idea of where they're succeeding and where they're struggling. (Of course, you always run into the person who has no idea where things are going sideways, and you will need to use different leadership tools to navigate that conversation.) It's our job as leaders to ask powerful questions and to listen with the intention of understanding, not with the intention of responding. This act shows our team that we're human, makes us more relatable, and demonstrates an authenticity that cannot be faked.

Once we've listened and have gained understanding of the successes, challenges, and barriers that team members face, we must take action: celebrate the wins, coach to overcome challenges, remove the barriers. As leaders, we must find a way to create an environment in which our team members can thrive. The results will follow.

Leveraging Empathy to Lead

One of the first times I realized I could use empathy as a strength in leading, involved a team member named Mary. She was always one of the first people into the office and the last person to leave. She was determined to do a good job, to prove her worth, and to show us that she added value. It only took a week of shifted hours, missed deadlines, and errors in her work for me to recognize that things were off, and it piqued my curiosity.

About halfway through her work term, I started to notice that she was making careless mistakes in her work. At first, I casually pointed them out as we were reviewing the work. I failed to notice how frustrating my feedback was to her, since I was doing it in a way that I thought was respectful. I was providing coaching and feedback on her performance, and she was digging in and doing more to show me that she was committed and dedicated. Around this time, I was developing the habit of reviewing my own development plan, and periodically refreshing myself on how to use my strengths in leadership. During my own reflection time, I decided to set up a meeting with Mary in a casual setting, where we could just get to know each other as people outside of the office and away from all of the tasks and duties of our jobs. It was over coffee with Mary that day that I truly got to witness the power of empathy in leadership.

I opened the conversation by asking her how she was doing. I didn't throw out that question lightly, and I made sure that my body language and tone matched my intention of the question. I truly wanted to know what she thought of the work, her performance, and our team. I was ready for the response, and I was going to listen actively to her words. She started off with the usual, "Oh I'm great, I'm really enjoying the work, and everything is fine." I asked her what she enjoyed about the work, what fine really meant, and if she felt fulfilled by the work. Through this open conversation, guided by my genuine curiosity to get to know this human being, I was able to uncover what was really going on beneath the surface, the 80% unseen part of Mary's life that was affecting the 20% of her life above the surface at work.

Mary had some serious family issues going on behind-the-scenes. Her family lived half-way across the country, she no support of her own, and she was unable to support her immediate family in the current situation. She wasn't sleeping or taking care of herself. She was deeply embarrassed by the fact that her personal life was affecting her professional life and thought that by pushing through, showing up, and doing more, she would be able to demonstrate that the negative aspects of her life were not affecting her. She thought she needed to separate the work life and the personal life, because that's what she had been told and believed to be true. Personal is personal, work is work, and never the two shall meet (which, we know now, is a load of garbage).

Mary wanted desperately for her work to go well so that she would have something to be proud of, but, in suppressing her personal experiences, the exact opposite happened. She wasn't doing a good job and was making mistakes in all her work. She wasn't patient, open-minded, or able to receive feedback.

She was tired, frustrated, and overwhelmed, and it showed in everything she did.

All of this came out in one 60-minute talk over a cup of coffee. Now that she had shared with me all that was going on in her life, I had a choice to make as to what I was going to do as her leader. Clearly, I couldn't offer much help in the family matters; however, I could offer support for herself. We talked about the importance of taking care of ourselves, especially in difficult times. She could see how neglecting herself during this time was affecting her ability to deliver the quality of work she was used to delivering. I told her to take the rest of the day off; go for a walk, spend some time in nature, let her mind clear, and forget about the work; rest, sleep, and rejuvenate. And she needed my permission as her leader to do this. Even if she knew already knew what to do, she needed my support. Otherwise, she never would have been able to leave the work at the office with a clear conscience and unplug. I knew that if she was able to come back with a clearer head, she would be able to get the deliverables done in no time. It was better for her to take a day off rather than stay and get a minimal amount of work done full of errors.

She came back the next day a different person. She had gone for a walk, talked to her family, spent time in her faith, attended a yoga class, and slept. Ultimately, she was able to take care of herself. That single act of meeting her where she needed to be met, bonded us in a way that will likely be a lifetime connection. My ability to be empathic, to put myself in her shoes, and really see and feel what she was going through, allowed me to make decisions as her leader that honored her and built a deep trusting connection. If you lead with empathy, the results will follow.

An Invitation to Be Truly Vulnerable

The more time I spend in the leadership space, the more I see people trying to keep on a mask of perfection that says, "I've got this gig all figured out and shame on you if you don't." The reality is that leading people is messy work that's constantly changing, because people are inherently messy and constantly changing. You should not expect people to show up any differently from how you yourself show up. We're complicated and complex, and that's okay. We don't need to hide from this truth.

If you never make a mistake or admit defeat, neither will your people. They will work so hard to cover up any imperfections that their energy will go into the cover-up of the mistakes, and not the heart of the work, which is exactly the opposite of what you require from them. If you never have a bad day and never talk about the difficulty of balancing your life with your career, your team will also try and emulate this quality. They will never bring forth their challenges, their issues with their families, or their aspirations that feel out of reach.

As high-performing people, we expect perfection. I have to work daily on overcoming this expectation for both myself and for others. Having high expectations and expecting perfection are closely related, but they are not the same. It's also our natural tendency as humans to assimilate to the environment around us. How do you want your team to show up? Are you doing your part to show them that being vulnerable, imperfect, and human is not only acceptable, but is required to be a part of your team?

In sharing our stories and the slices of ourselves that are relevant to the situation, we build trust. In building trust, we break down barriers and advance our workplaces, whether this is a 1,000-person corporation in a metropolis downtown, or two moms around a kitchen table in small town suburbia. We must be willing to share ourselves in order to lift each other up, connect, and truly reach our fullest potential as a team.

Some of the moments I've learned the most, were moments when I was able to say:

"Can you show me more? I don't know much about XYZ."
"I had a similar situation happen to me once. Would it be okay for me to share with you what I learned?"
"I have also experienced XYZ. This is a tough time you are navigating. What can I do to support you through it?"

Notice that none of these statements require to you to dump out your guts or open up your heart. You only have to be willing to see what this other person is going through and offer your support. You have to be willing to say that you don't have all the answers, and invite someone to teach you about what they know. You have to be willing to be vulnerable and to peel back the mask of perfection, and admit that you don't know. You have to show that you are willing to sit in a messy, uncertain situation with another imperfect, whole human being and figure it out together.

CHAPTER 12: EMPATHY FOR SELF

*"Self-compassion is key because when we're able to be gentle
with ourselves in the midst of shame, we're more likely to
reach out, connect, and experience empathy."*
—Brene Brown, *Scholar, Author, Speaker*

If the definition of empathy is the ability to see and understand emotions in others, does it not stand to reason that we can have empathy for ourselves, to see and understand our own emotions? From the beginning of my journey in understanding empathy, I have always found it easier to see and understand others' emotions. What blindsides me are my own emotions, thoughts, and feelings.

Writing this book has been an entire exercise in self-compassion. Inviting people to share in my work and sharing my thoughts, experiences, and learning while receiving feedback, edits, and criticism is incredibly humbling. I can say that I've never had a more vulnerable experience. Learning about me—my emotions, my thoughts, and my beliefs—started with assessments (a most fortunate accident that I'm deeply grateful for). You may choose to start there, but your journey may start somewhere else. Ultimately, the understanding I have of myself today is a culmination of assessments, training, feedback, coaching, and personal exploration.

The assessments gave me awareness of behavioral tendencies and personality traits, and gave me language to communicate with my team. Training and implementation of the concepts has increased and enhanced my skills in leadership, communication, and active listening. Accepting feedback from my team members and leaders has allowed me to enhance others' experiences while working with me. Coaching has forced me look at my belief patterns, and has helped me build the capabilities needed to operate from a place with less fear, less judgment, and more curiosity. Personal exploration has allowed me to check in with myself, to take stock of where I'm at and how I'm doing, and to make the necessary adjustments. Meditation, journaling, and reflection has granted me the ability to hear and feel my own genuine GPS, allowing me to stay on track and show up as the person I know I am.

The resources section at the end of the book has suggestions for assessments, books, and training. While this is nowhere near a comprehensive or complete list of everything that available, they are my favorites and are a good place to start. If you are working in an organization and have access to internal leadership training, go for it! Step up, say yes, and see where it takes you.

Personal Exploration

Honestly, this could be an entire book on its own. That being said, to practice empathy in your life, you'll need to start a practice of self-exploration, and it will have to be suited to you. I use a combination of floating, meditation, yoga, journaling, and writing. It will be as unique for you as your fingerprint. I suggest you approach exploring yourself as a bit of an experiment, and give yourself permission to try on a number of techniques for a month and then see what you like, what worked, and what just didn't land for you. I can't give you a one-size-fits-all solution, because it doesn't exist; you will need to do the work.

If you're really stuck and just can't move forward, start by getting a coach. Work on the one thing that's causing the most discomfort in your life at this current moment. Just like we need a fitness coach to help us push past the discomfort and allow our physical bodies to strengthen, a development coach can help you strengthen muscles and build capabilities that will allow you to move forward in your life.

Be open to making mistakes, so that you can create a culture where mistakes are seen as failing forward and not life threatening. Let your team learn together. Resist the urge to jump in and fix it, and to have things done your way. Let your team find new, innovative, and possibly game-changing solutions to the current challenge.

Just as you need to meet people where they are, most people will try and meet you where you set the bar. Remember that expectations bar we talked about earlier in Chapter 6? Check in to see where your bar is set (daily or even hourly). Is it attainable, or is it so far out of reach that it's demotivating and discouraging? Or is it so low that no one will be challenged and will only give 50% of themselves, breeding resentment and disengagement?

What are your expectations? How open are you to other people's ways of doing things, their ideas, and their contributions? Are you up to the task of coaching, supporting, and delegating to your team members as they are ready for it?

Being an empath is a tricky space to navigate. On one hand, you gain valuable insights and can build trust at lighting speeds, because you can meet someone where they are and truly understand and feel what it is like to be them. On the other hand, it can be exhausting and overwhelming taking on all the emotional baggage from those around you, especially if you feel responsible for their experience. The amount of energy and ongoing attention required to truly be empathic can be draining. You'll need to make sure you have a plan and take the time to rest, recharge, and rejuvenate yourself. If you don't, you run the risk of getting depleted and burning out.

Preventing Burnout

What does burnout look like? Well, here's what it looks like for me: feeling tired, impatience with everyone and everything, inflexibility, physical illness, insomnia, and emotional outbursts. That last one really hurts to admit, but it's the honest truth.

I'm going to go back into my early days a leader, even as far back as when I was a kid trying to lead in my family. I really believed that if I had a sound plan, people would naturally do what I asked them to do. When this didn't happen or, God forbid, my plan failed or didn't yield the results I thought it should, I was overcome with emotion. I couldn't understand this and had very limited language to describe what it was or how it felt. I would also have physical manifestations *(elevated heart rate, shortness of breath, and crying without warning)* of the stress and anguish I was feeling. Often, an outburst would happen at the most inopportune times. I've been known to be that woman crying in the boss's office, and I've had health issues *(insomnia, upset stomach, increased appetite, decreased energy level, and interruptions of my monthly cycle)* that were all stress-related.

What I know now is that, when I was first learning, I didn't have the skills or insight to link all of the pieces together. For the first decade of my career, the only piece of constructive criticism I received in my annual performance review was to work on fixing the over-emotional part of me. No one ever offered guidance outside of trying to leave that part of me at home, and so I tried for years to push my emotions down, to leave them at home, to toughen up, and to stop caring so much. I tried desperately to be able to get a hold of myself during conflict or heated discussions, which often meant that I stayed silent. I could never master any of these skills, and by the end of 2011, I had arrived at the conclusion that maybe I just wasn't cut out to work in this man's world, and that I had made a huge mistake in my career choice. But I had no idea where to go next or what to do about this realization.

Driven by a sense of duty and pride (after all, I am not one who gives up on things easily), I hung in there. I realized that these outbursts, and my lack of patience, where really symptoms of a much deeper issue. I was burnt out. I had nothing left to give in those moments, no capacity to hear, no words to communicate what was going on, and no understanding of the root cause. Burnout. Having grown up in a family that lived and breathed the serenity prayer, I decided that I would work on changing the only thing I knew I could change: me.

Here are just a few things that I learned about how to effectively leverage the empath in me and overcome burnout.

> **Challenge:** I only knew how to put myself at the bottom of my priority list. I would plan time to rest and recharge, but I was totally ineffective at following through and actually holding that space in my schedule as a priority. If anyone made a request for my time or needed me for something, I would willingly give up my "me time" in order to help them out. I failed to realize that there was a cost to doing this, and I would find myself slowly sliding down the slippery path of being burnt out and overwhelmed.

> **Solution:** I now try (I'm still working on making it automatic) to say, "I would love to be able to help

out, but let me check my schedule and get back to you." This does a couple of things: it helps me honor my desire to help, and it allows me to assess whether or not I want to give this time. I can slow down and make a conscious choice about who, how, and when I give the hours of my day. It also helps me make myself a priority. (This practice has been an essential part of finishing this book.)

Challenge: I would take on other people's emotions as my own and feel responsible for them.

Over the past five years, I began to understand that if I found myself in a conversation with a team member, boss, or family member, I would always take responsibility for how everyone was feeling during and after the conversation. I couldn't separate my own emotions from theirs, and it left me overwhelmed with feelings I couldn't sort out. I didn't know why I felt this way or where it came from.

Solution: I learned that in order to avoid getting mixed up with other people's emotions, I had to get clear on my own emotions. One of the most powerful tools I've found is floating, which may be a new idea for some of you. Floating is, at its core, sensory deprivation therapy. My coach/therapist/ mentor suggested it when I found myself with Friday nights off from all duties of marriage, motherhood, and career, when I literally had no idea what to do with myself. I didn't know how to sit and just be with myself, in my physical body or in my mind. I found myself running errands and checking items off the to-do lists, which got a lot done. However, it didn't leave me feeling more in touch with myself or my feelings. Floating is meditation, rest, detoxification, and relaxation all wrapped up in a pod of warm salt water!

Floating is done inside a light-proof, sound-proof float pod, which is pitch black and completely quiet. There is 10-12 inches of high salinity water (think the dead sea) set to body temperature. I usually float for 60 minutes but have done floats as long as two and a half hours; that's 150 minutes of no interruptions, no external stimuli, no forces of gravity pulling on my physical body. Just me, myself, and I, getting to know one another. Honestly, it's pure magic, and I hope you give it a try.

Challenge: I couldn't just "be." Many coaches and mentors have told me just "be." What does this mean, anyway? Well, what finally got through to me was the analogy of a tree. Trees are just trees. A pine tree is a pine tree—not an oak tree, not a willow tree, just a pine tree. A robin is a robin. It lays blue eggs, catches worms in the rain, and is really happy being a robin. Everything in nature is exactly what it is and nothing else. What I realized is that things in nature are happy and content in being what they are.

Human beings, on the other hand, are usually trying to be something else, something that someone told us we should be, or something that we heard we should do or try. Very few of us are taught to be who we are and encouraged to just be ourselves. From small children, we are encouraged to try new things, to carry on the family business, or walk the path our parents have walked, when, in reality, we are all unique individuals with our own unique purpose to fulfill. Why then don't we spend time getting to know ourselves, our passions, our purpose, and just be?

Solution: Pay attention to what makes you happy. How do you want to spend each day? Now, I know there are arguments for both sides here, begging questions about, "What if I can't make money?" or, "How can I make a living doing this?" but stay with me a little longer. For me, I love connected conversations with people and helping them see, discover, and grow into the person they always knew they wanted to be. Working as an engineer, dealing mostly with inanimate objects, wasn't a great fit for me. I could do it, but I wasn't able to be my true self in that role.

If you're like me and a little impatient, you will want to turn your ship 180 degrees in a few minutes to chart your new course as soon as you discover it. Pay attention, tune in, and start to chart a new course, but don't rush. Imagine you are trying to turn the Titanic. You need a sense of urgency, as in there's an iceberg (i.e., the leader you don't want to be) ahead which you need to steer clear of, and you know that this fully-loaded ship (i.e., the person you currently are) will not turn on a dime. It takes time, careful planning, constant monitoring, and sometimes trusting in the invisible and letting our inner self guide us for a while.

The bottom line is that, in order to be an empathic leader effectively, you need to make yourself a priority. You need to stay rested, recharged, and relaxed. You need to be fully present with yourself so that you can be fully present with others. You will need to know, understand, and accept your own emotions, to have space to hold others separate from you.

A Test or a Sign?

Do you ever feel like the world is giving you signs that you are heading in the right direction, or maybe the wrong direction? I have a deeply-held belief that if I paid close enough attention and looked for the signs, the answers to my universal questions would be provided, but, recently, I had to challenge this belief. What if the very thing we think is a sign is actually a test to see if we've learned the lesson, and to show us that we do have the strength and skills to do something different? For me, it was a test to see if I was ready to make myself a priority, when everything in my life seemed to say that others needed me more.

I consistently have trouble letting other people help me, and taking time to take care of myself. Some would classify me as a highly ambitious, Type A mother of three who doesn't know how to sit still. But deep inside of me, there's a person longing for stillness, quiet, and peaceful reflection. These two parts of my life are often at odds with each other. I found myself in the midst of a war between these two parts of my being, as I prepared to leave for three nights on a girls' getaway weekend and leave my family alone to fend for themselves. I'll preface this by saying, Matthew is a highly capable father and routinely manages the household and children's activities on his own with great success. After decades of marriage, I realized that it's me who has difficulty letting go and creating space for him.

As I was preparing to leave work on Wednesday evening, due to fly out at 10 am the next morning, I felt like life was closing in on me. In this moment, I remember thinking to myself that this was a sign. I found myself thinking: "This is the sign, Erin, that you should not be going on this trip. The soccer schedule just came out, the boys have two events a day, and it will be tough for Matthew to manage on his own. What makes you think you get to go to the spa and have all of this time alone for yourself, and leave him here to fend for three kids and to deal with all the things that are going to come up? You've got a ton of approvals to get through at work, and there's no way you can leave this for the next couple of days."

I'm sure you can relate and have found yourself in a similar thought pattern in similar situations. And for a few hours on Wednesday evening, every time I turned around, there was yet another sign telling me that I couldn't get away and that I shouldn't be doing this girls' trip or taking this time for myself; it was just too much to ask. As I was drifting off to sleep on Wednesday night, feeling anxious and being very negative with myself, it suddenly hit me. What if this is actually just a test to see if I can put myself first?

I've been neglecting myself since I was a child. Over the years, I've gotten glimpses of what it's like when you take care of yourself, but I've been spotty at best. I never found a consistent or sustainable way to take care of myself until recently. As I drifted off to sleep that Wednesday evening, and contemplated the thought of signs in our lives versus tests in our lives, I felt a peacefulness settle over me like I have never felt before.

I woke up on Thursday morning ready to ace this exam. Of course my husband can manage the kids; he's been doing it for years, and he's never let us down once. Check. Of course work will be fine. I can leave for 48 hours, and the project isn't going to fall apart; I have capable people on my team who have my back. Check. Of course I deserve this time, and it's up to me to make it happen. Check.

As I sit here looking back at this experience, I'm extremely proud of myself for passing the test. It was not easy on anyone. It wasn't easy to leave. It wasn't easy on the ones I left behind to run life when I took some time do a little self-reflection. But not being easy and not being possible are two entirely different things. In order for people to step up and help us out, we have to create space for them to do so, and creating space means stepping back. It means letting go and loosening the grip.

Give yourself permission to ask for help. Speaking as someone who needed an army of assistance getting to this point in my life, you might need some to engage different people, resources, and support. Developing skills and practices in your life is hard, messy work. Identifying new possibilities and building sustainable capabilities to reach these new possibilities, takes dedication and accountability. But I know you can do it.

CHAPTER 13: BE TRUE TO NOW

"Right where you are is where you need to be. Don't fight it!
Don't run away from it! Stand firm! Take a deep breath. And
another. And another. Now ask yourself: Why is this in my
world? What do I need to see?"
—Iyanla Vanzant, *Author, Speaker,*
TV Personality, Lawyer, Life Coach

My final and deepest desire for you is to trust in the process. You are right where you need to be. Remain open to evolution and opportunity. Decide to ditch competition and comparison.

We can build the best plans, knowing that the journey to reach the destination will look nothing like that plan. The journey is designed to teach us what we need to know, so that when we reach the destination, we have the tools required to stay there.

There are many seasons to life. There will be times when it will be just you and your career, and you can operate at a different pace and schedule than the season when you have family commitments. This might be a spouse, children, siblings, or aging parents, all of whom will demand your time and attention.

Once, I was driving my family home after an extended family celebration, reflecting on the weekend and looking forward to the week ahead, when we drove past a golf course. I made a comment that it was unfortunate that the course was shut down, and wondered why it had closed. My kids remarked that it must be very old as it didn't look much like a golf course, and Matthew replied that it had only been a couple of seasons since it shut down. I spent the next three hours driving as my family slept in the car, my mind processing this observation of how quickly mother nature was taking back this abandoned golf course. Without maintenance and human interference, the course was returning to the forested landscape surrounding it.

And I wondered if this is true for us human beings as well. Do we revert to our natural state when we stop maintaining ourselves? What if we give up on some of the maintenance we do on ourselves? How do you know what's required and what's not? And why do we work so hard to maintain appearances, which don't serve who we really are or who we really want to be? I understand maintaining my hair color, the shape of my eyebrows, and the strength in my muscles. I understand keeping our homes in good repair so that they last as long as possible.

What I don't understand is, why we try and force ourselves in to jobs and careers that don't fit. Why do we live in houses and drive cars that don't reflect who we truly are? Why do we wear clothes only to follow the current runway fashion trends, even though we can't stand leggings, loose pants, long shirts, or whatever the current trend is? Have you ever noticed that the most beautiful places, spaces, and people are those which most closely resemble their most natural selves, requiring minimal or even undetectable maintenance?

Is it easier to maintain something which closely resembles its natural state? If the maintained version of something closely resembles the natural state, is maintenance merely enhancing the natural beauty? Does it take as much effort? I spent three hours pondering these thoughts without arriving at an answer.

But here's where I did arrive. As humans, we are creative creatures looking to enhance ourselves and our surroundings. So, how do we see our true surroundings and our true selves, so that we enhance the natural beauty, instead of covering it up or changing it so completely, that we lose sight of what was there in the beginning?

In 2013, the city where I live experienced the worst flood in 100 years. The river ran right downtown and flowed deep from within in the Rocky Mountains to the west of us, but, over the years, had been diverted making way for developments. In less than 24 hours, the raw force of mother nature returned the landscape to her original form. Houses were ripped apart, golf courses were devastated, bridges were torn down, highways washed away like they had never even existed.

If we keep pushing, moving further and further away from the very essence of who we are, from our natural form, we will at some point be faced with the force of nature, that will force us to return to our natural state and embrace our true self.

We can build lives, relationships, and careers however we want to, in whatever vision we have for ourselves. However, the further our lives, relationships, and careers deviate from our natural form, the more maintenance they will require, taking more and more emotional and physical effort to keep things looking good and functioning well. And the larger our deviation is from our natural form, the larger the devastation is, requiring more time and energy to repair once the reckoning forces ultimately return us to ourselves.

After close to 40 years on this earth, in my three-hour drive that day, I found examples in lives, careers, and relationships of this very reckoning in my small sphere of existence. The further away from what should naturally be, the more effort it takes to maintain it, and the bigger the shake up is when the world tries to right itself. Four years post-flood, we still haven't finished the clean-up and rebuilding of the city and surrounding areas.

What's your natural order? In what ways are you living close to your natural order, and in what ways do you need to look at moving closer to it? What feels hard in your life? What feels like it needs your constant attention, more than just a loving check-in to maintain? The more we shift toward our own natural order of being, the more ease and grace we will experience, the more energy we will have, and the more enjoyment we will draw from our everyday experiences.

Each of us must find our own natural order. No two people are the same, so it will look different for each and every one of us. In a world where we compare and compete, strive to achieve, and are constantly connected with each other, it can be very hard to hear our own rhythms, to see our own beauty, and to find our own natural order. Perhaps it will take a friend, a family member, a psychologist, a coach, some time alone, a walk in nature, daily meditations, trying something new, or some magic combination of all of these, but I believe it is time well spent and a journey worth venturing out to explore.

You don't have to say yes to every opportunity that comes your way, nor should you shut it down right away. If I've learned anything in my time on earth, it's that you need to learn to swim in the muddy waters. Learn to embrace uncertainty, for therein lies the opportunity to create something new. The best things in my life have happened when I've least expected them to, and I certainly didn't have them planned. Let yourself evolve, stay present with yourself, and be curious about life.

CONCLUSION

Thank you for being a part of my journey with me. I set out to provide you with a glimpse into my own leadership journey thus far, and to offer you some how-to practical suggestions to implement in your own life. I hope that is what you found, and that you have gained a deeper appreciation for and understanding of what leading with empathy looks like, and the impact it can have.

One person may not be able to change the world. I equate sharing my story and my learnings about leading with more heart, more connection, and deep empathy to a stone dropped in water. That stone, my story, will send out ripples across the waters to unknown places. I am excited to see what lies ahead. I hope if you've learned something, or if a story has touched you, that you share your experience with me and those closest to you. If you know of someone who would benefit from reading these pages, I hope you share the book.

Most of all, I hope that each and every person works at becoming better acquainted with themselves. Our weaknesses hold no power over us when we bring them into the daylight. Our strength lies in our ability to embrace our differences.

I believe from the depths of my soul that I can play a part in changing the leadership experience in my own generation and generations to come, and so can you. Together, we can achieve greatness.

RESOURCES

The links to all of these resources can be found on my website at www.insideoutempathy.com/resources

ASSESSMENTS

There are literally thousands of assessments you could complete. Start slow and make sure you take the time after each one to integrate the information it's providing you. This is not a "check the box" exercise. It's not quantity over quality. Each assessment provides you with another piece of information about yourself, and you will need to decide what to do with it. Does it fit? Is it accurate?

DiSC
www.discprofile.com

Meyer's Briggs
www.16personalities.com/free-personality-test

Strength Finders 2.0

www.gallupstrengthscenter.com

TRAINING

Start by looking into your company's available training. Exhaust what they have to offer, remembering to implement the top two or three key points from each session.

If you still want more in the way of classroom or facilitated learning, I recommend the Situational Leadership II and 7 Habits of Highly Effective People courses. These are for everyone, leader or not. Combined, these two courses provide a powerful framework to guide you, as a leader or team member, through your growth and development.

Situational Leadership II
https://www.kenblanchard.com/Events-Workshops/
Workshops?Topic=Situational-Leadership-II

7 Habits of Highly Effective People
https://www.franklincovey.com/Solutions/Leadership/7-habits-signature.html

RECOMMENDED READING

Where do I even start?! I'm a book junkie and voracious reader, but I've tried to narrow it down to my favorite books which have impacted and shaped my life. This list will change rapidly—I read a lot! Please check out my website for the most current, up to date list at www.insideoutempathy.com/resources

On Leading Others

One Minute Manager - Spencer Johnson, Ken Blanchard and Spencer M. D. Johnson

Gung Ho - Ken Blanchard and Sheldon M. Bowles

Good To Great - James C. Collins

On Leading Self

Gifts of Imperfections - Brene Brown

Lean In - Sheryl Sandburg and Nell Scovell

7 Habits of Highly Effective People - Stephen Covey

Slight Edge - Jeff Olson and John David Mann

What to Say When You Talk to Yourself - Shad Helmstetter

Strength Finders 2.0 - Tom Rath

Emotional Intelligence 2.0 - Travis Bradberry and Jean Greaves

Daring Greatly - Brene Brown

Rookie Smarts - Liz Wiseman

Play Big - Tara Mohr

Rising Strong - Brene Brown

Braving the Wilderness - Brene Brown

ACKNOWLEDGEMENTS

This book has been a labor of love, and there were days I honestly thought it wouldn't happen. In some aspects it felt like birthing a child, and in others the endeavor has taken more from me than I ever imagine. It would not have been possible without the following people who have supported, guided, cheered and picked me up along the way.

Thank you to the many teachers, coaches, mentors, sponsors, team members and leaders I've been fortunate enough to encounter so far—I cannot name each of you by name, but know that you are thought of and honored for your contribution to my life.

To the team that made this all possible at Paper Raven Books—Morgan, Victoria, Sarah, Darcy, Jesus, Michael, and Amanda—you all make magic happen! Thank you for your thoughtful feedback, insightful guidance, gentle (and sometimes not so gentle) nudging along, and your tireless efforts in bringing this book to life. Thank you!

To my parents for loving me enough to accept all parts of me, even the ones that aren't so beautiful or polished. Thank you for letting me make mistakes and fail forward. For giving our family roots, each of us wings to fly and a safe place to land, I love you.

To my sisters, Danielle and Lesley, and my brother, John, you were my first teachers, my first team! Watching you grow up, set out in the world, and build your own families has been a truly amazing experience for me. Thank you for supporting me unconditionally.

To my husband, Matthew, and our children, Olivia, Henry and Thomas—you are my home team! Thank you for choosing me to share your lives with. Thank you for teaching me more about myself every day and allowing me a safe place to learn and grow. Your support of not only this book, but of all of my wild and crazy ideas, means the world to me. I love you.

27637608R00148

Made in the USA
Lexington, KY
06 January 2019